D0949475

NATIONAL SECURITY

NATIONAL SECURITY

Other books in the At Issue series:

NATIONAL SECURITY

Laura K. Egendorf, *Book Editor*

Daniel Leone, *President*
Bonnie Szumski, *Publisher*
Scott Barbour, *Managing Editor*

GREENHAVEN
PRESS ®

San Diego • Detroit • New York • San Francisco • Cleveland
New Haven, Conn. • Waterville, Maine • London • Munich

© 2003 by Greenhaven Press. Greenhaven Press is an imprint of The Gale Group, Inc., a division of Thomson Learning, Inc.

Greenhaven® and Thomson Learning™ are trademarks used herein under license.

For more information, contact
Greenhaven Press
27500 Drake Rd.
Farmington Hills, MI 48331-3535
Or you can visit our Internet site at http://www.gale.com

LIBRARY OF CONGRESS CATALOGING-IN-PUBLICATION DATA

National security / Laura K. Egendorf, book editor.
    p. cm. — (At issue)
  Includes bibliographical references and index.
  ISBN 0-7377-1428-X (pbk. : alk. paper) — ISBN 0-7377-1427-1 (lib. : alk. paper)
    1. National security—United States. 2. United States—Defenses. I. Egendorf, Laura K., 1973– . II. At issue (San Diego, Calif.)
  UA23 .N247724 2003
  355'.033073—dc21   2002027155

Printed in the United States of America

Contents

Introduction

On September 11, 2001, America's sense of security crumbled. Terrorists, using commercial airplanes as missiles, destroyed the World Trade Center buildings in New York City and caused serious damage to the Pentagon in Arlington, Virginia, while a third plane, targeted for either the White House or the Capitol, crashed in a Pennsylvania field. More than three thousand people died in what was by far the worst terrorist attack on U.S. soil.

In the wake of September 11, questions have been raised as to what steps the United States should take to prevent further terrorist attacks and ensure national security. Naturally, the U.S. military has figured strongly in these discussions. Many suggestions for enhancing the military's effectiveness against terrorism have focused on military spending.

William J. Taylor, a retired colonel and former director of national security studies at West Point, is among those who argue that the American military will not be able to fight the war against terrorism without sizable increases in defense spending. According to Taylor, the military's numerous missions throughout Europe and Asia have left it "underfunded and overstretched." Many military units are unavailable for missions in Afghanistan, where the United States has been fighting a war against the Taliban—the Islamic fundamentalist regime that ruled Afghanistan and harbored Osama bin Laden and the al-Qaeda terrorist network, the people allegedly responsible for the September 11 attacks. In addition, some of the military units that are available are not prepared yet for hostile situations in the mountains of Afghanistan. Taylor writes: "If America is truly serious about a multiyear war against terrorism—with a whole host of new military requirements implied—the powers that be in Washington need to 'belly up to the bar' and make the case for maintaining military capabilities."

Other writers contend that the military must have enough resources to fight terrorism without outside help. In an article for the *National Review*, Mark Helprin asserts that the United States cannot wholly depend on Middle Eastern allies in its battles in Afghanistan. For example, nations surrounding the Persian Gulf could demand that U.S. forces leave their lands. He writes, "The way around [these problems] is simple and traditional—to possess the massive military power the United States can afford, and to use it either to achieve decisive victories or to force capitulation without a shot." He argues against cuts in the size of the B-1 bomber fleet and contends that the United States should return to its policy of being prepared for two simultaneous wars.

However, if national security is to be strengthened, military spending must also be increased for homeland defense, many argue. Admiral James M. Loy, in a speech to the conservative think tank Heritage Foundation, asserts that the Coast Guard is essential to homeland security. For example, the Coast Guard can protect America's maritime industries and its major ports by inspecting cargo shipments for contraband weapons and technology. He also cites the Coast Guard's experience with providing disaster relief and its status as both a federal law enforcement agency and military branch as reasons why it is "uniquely positioned among federal agencies to fight an enemy that crosses boundaries with seeming impunity." Loy suggests that the Coast Guard's efforts could be strengthened with the help of new equipment, including gamma-ray scanners and high-technology sensors, which would be used to survey cargo and ensure that dangerous materials would not enter the country.

Another way that the military's ability to protect national security could be improved is to enhance its intelligence gathering capabilities. Although most people associate intelligence gathering (and its reported failures in connection to the September 11 attacks) with the CIA and FBI, much of the work is done by military agencies, in particular the National Security Agency and the National Reconnaissance Office. Many experts argue that military intelligence agencies should be under the auspices of a chief executive who has real budgetary power and is not just a figurehead. As the editors of the British magazine *Economist* contend, "'Reforming' America's intelligence services is not simply a matter of getting better people and giving them more money and a slightly freer hand. The structure needs modernising from top to bottom." The article states that these agencies will need a massive equipment upgrade, including new satellites and computer systems, if they are to successfully protect national security. Other writers have suggested allocating more money toward covert human intelligence—agents who can infiltrate enemy nations and help the military understand and analyze the information gathered by its satellites and imagery equipment.

In contrast, many commentators maintain that simply throwing more money at the military is not the answer. Many analysts argue that the military needs to completely change its mission and adapt to the current world situation. In an article for the *Harvard International Review*, Gregory D. Foster, a professor at the National Defense University in Washington, D.C., suggests that the military of the future should be "designed primarily for peacekeeping, nation-building, humanitarian assistance, and disaster response." Foster maintains that in order to achieve these goals, the military needs to de-emphasize traditional hierarchies, allow for more democracy in decision making, and employ better-educated and older personnel.

Indeed, many observers believe that the military should not be so dependent on a continually increasing budget. Harvey M. Sapolsky and Eugene Gholz, professors at the Massachusetts Institute of Technology and the University of Kentucky respectively, suggest that the best way to encourage military innovation is to place a cap on spending; for example, the military budget for the war against the al-Qaeda terrorist network should be limited to $350 billion per year. They write: "A budget ceiling gives participants in the war effort a constraint against which to value their efforts. The measure of everything becomes the likely contribution to victory." Restricting the military's budget would compel the Pentagon to look for solutions beyond buying pricey, but not always reliable, equipment. Sapolsky and Gholz suggest that only a few billion dollars—to fund special operation forces and purchase precision-guided weapons—is needed for the defense industry to adequately protect homeland security. A ceiling would also force the military to set priorities by focusing on clearer threats and could encourage competition and innovation among the different branches of the military.

In its paper "U.S. Military Transformation: Not Just More Spending, But Better Spending" the Center for Defense Information (CDI) also argues in favor of more focused spending. CDI lists fifteen programs that the Pentagon should cancel or reduce—such as the building of nuclear warheads, aircraft carriers, and the B-1B Lancer Bomber—in order to save at least $147 billion in ten years. By making these cuts, the Pentagon will free "funding and people-power for the war on terrorism and other potential military requirements of the 21st century."

The U.S. military is a central player in the preservation of national security and the execution of the war against terrorism. However, national security is an issue that involves numerous government agencies, from the Justice Department to the Immigration and Naturalization Service, and private industries. A variety of steps have been taken by these entities since September 11, 2001, many of which have inspired debate about their effectiveness and their constitutionality. In *At Issue: National Security*, the authors debate how the world's largest democracy can best protect its citizens.

1

The United States Must Fight Terrorism to Ensure National Security

George W. Bush

George W. Bush is the forty-third president of the United States.

Regardless of the actions of other nations, America must do all it can to fight terrorism and guarantee national security. Although the war on terrorism is difficult and dangerous, America and its allies will continue to fight it. Nations that are hostile to the United States, or that are too timid to join the coalition, must recognize that America will do anything necessary to ensure its security. Among these efforts are increasing the defense budget, strengthening police and fire departments, and improving airport security and border control. America must continue to stand for liberty and freedom.

Thank you very much. Mr. Speaker, Vice President Cheney, members of Congress, distinguished guests, fellow citizens: As we gather tonight, our nation is at war, our economy is in recession, and the civilized world faces unprecedented dangers. Yet the state of our Union has never been stronger.

We last met in an hour of shock and suffering. In four short months [since the September 11 terrorist attacks on America], our nation has comforted the victims, begun to rebuild New York and the Pentagon, rallied a great coalition, captured, arrested, and rid the world of thousands of terrorists, destroyed Afghanistan's terrorist training camps, saved a people from starvation, and freed a country from brutal oppression. The American flag flies again over our embassy in Kabul. Terrorists who once occupied Afghanistan now occupy cells at Guantanamo Bay. And terrorist leaders who urged followers to sacrifice their lives are running for their own.

America and Afghanistan are now allies against terror. We'll be partners in rebuilding that country. And this evening we welcome the distinguished interim leader of a liberated Afghanistan: Chairman Hamid

Excerpted from George W. Bush's State of the Union address, January 29, 2002.

Karzai. The last time we met in this chamber, the mothers and daughters of Afghanistan were captives in their own homes, forbidden from working or going to school. Today women are free, and are part of Afghanistan's new government. And we welcome the new Minister of Women's Affairs, Doctor Sima Samar. Our progress is a tribute to the spirit of the Afghan people, to the resolve of our coalition, and to the might of the United States military. When I called our troops into action, I did so with complete confidence in their courage and skill. And tonight, thanks to them, we are winning the war on terror. The men and women of our Armed Forces have delivered a message now clear to every enemy of the United States: Even 7,000 miles away, across oceans and continents, on mountaintops and in caves—you will not escape the justice of this nation.

For many Americans, these four months have brought sorrow, and pain that will never completely go away. Every day a retired firefighter returns to Ground Zero, to feel closer to his two sons who died there. At a memorial in New York, a little boy left his football with a note for his lost father: "Dear Daddy, please take this to heaven. I don't want to play football until I can play with you again some day."

[In December 2001,] at the grave of her husband, Michael, a CIA officer and Marine who died in Mazur-e-Sharif, Shannon Spann said these words of farewell: "Semper Fi, my love." Shannon is with us tonight.

Shannon, I assure you and all who have lost a loved one that our cause is just, and our country will never forget the debt we owe Michael and all who gave their lives for freedom.

Our cause is just, and it continues. Our discoveries in Afghanistan confirmed our worst fears, and showed us the true scope of the task ahead. We have seen the depth of our enemies' hatred in videos, where they laugh about the loss of innocent life. And the depth of their hatred is equaled by the madness of the destruction they design. We have found diagrams of American nuclear power plants and public water facilities, detailed instructions for making chemical weapons, surveillance maps of American cities, and thorough descriptions of landmarks in America and throughout the world.

What we have found in Afghanistan confirms that, far from ending there, our war against terror is only beginning. Most of the 19 men who hijacked planes on September the 11th were trained in Afghanistan's camps, and so were tens of thousands of others. Thousands of dangerous killers, schooled in the methods of murder, often supported by outlaw regimes, are now spread throughout the world like ticking time bombs, set to go off without warning.

America will remain steadfast

Thanks to the work of our law enforcement officials and coalition partners, hundreds of terrorists have been arrested. Yet, tens of thousands of trained terrorists are still at large. These enemies view the entire world as a battlefield, and we must pursue them wherever they are. So long as training camps operate, so long as nations harbor terrorists, freedom is at risk. And America and our allies must not, and will not, allow it.

Our nation will continue to be steadfast and patient and persistent in the pursuit of two great objectives. First, we will shut down terrorist camps, disrupt terrorist plans, and bring terrorists to justice. And, second, we must prevent the terrorists and regimes who seek chemical, biological or nuclear weapons from threatening the United States and the world.

Our military has put the terror training camps of Afghanistan out of business, yet camps still exist in at least a dozen countries. A terrorist underworld—including groups like Hamas, Hezbollah, Islamic Jihad, Jaish-i-Mohammed—operates in remote jungles and deserts, and hides in the centers of large cities.

> *Some governments will be timid in the face of terror.*
> *. . . If they do not act, America will.*

While the most visible military action is in Afghanistan, America is acting elsewhere. We now have troops in the Philippines, helping to train that country's armed forces to go after terrorist cells that have executed an American, and still hold hostages. Our soldiers, working with the Bosnian government, seized terrorists who were plotting to bomb our embassy. Our Navy is patrolling the coast of Africa to block the shipment of weapons and the establishment of terrorist camps in Somalia.

My hope is that all nations will heed our call, and eliminate the terrorist parasites who threaten their countries and our own. Many nations are acting forcefully. Pakistan is now cracking down on terror, and I admire the strong leadership of President Musharraf.

But some governments will be timid in the face of terror. And make no mistake about it: If they do not act, America will.

Opposing terrorist regimes

Our second goal is to prevent regimes that sponsor terror from threatening America or our friends and allies with weapons of mass destruction. Some of these regimes have been pretty quiet since September the 11th. But we know their true nature. North Korea is a regime arming with missiles and weapons of mass destruction, while starving its citizens.

Iran aggressively pursues these weapons and exports terror, while an unelected few repress the Iranian people's hope for freedom.

Iraq continues to flaunt its hostility toward America and to support terror. The Iraqi regime has plotted to develop anthrax, and nerve gas, and nuclear weapons for over a decade. This is a regime that has already used poison gas to murder thousands of its own citizens—leaving the bodies of mothers huddled over their dead children. This is a regime that agreed to international inspections—then kicked out the inspectors. This is a regime that has something to hide from the civilized world.

States like these, and their terrorist allies, constitute an axis of evil, arming to threaten the peace of the world. By seeking weapons of mass destruction, these regimes pose a grave and growing danger. They could provide these arms to terrorists, giving them the means to match their hatred. They could attack our allies or attempt to blackmail the United States. In any of these cases, the price of indifference would be catastrophic.

We will work closely with our coalition to deny terrorists and their state sponsors the materials, technology, and expertise to make and deliver weapons of mass destruction. We will develop and deploy effective missile defenses to protect America and our allies from sudden attack. And all nations should know: America will do what is necessary to ensure our nation's security.

We'll be deliberate, yet time is not on our side. I will not wait on events, while dangers gather. I will not stand by, as peril draws closer and closer. The United States of America will not permit the world's most dangerous regimes to threaten us with the world's most destructive weapons.

Our war on terror is well begun, but it is only begun. This campaign may not be finished on our watch—yet it must be and it will be waged on our watch. We can't stop short. If we stop now—leaving terror camps intact and terror states unchecked—our sense of security would be false and temporary. History has called America and our allies to action, and it is both our responsibility and our privilege to fight freedom's fight.

Three important goals

Our first priority must always be the security of our nation, and that will be reflected in the budget I send to Congress. My budget supports three great goals for America: We will win this war; we'll protect our homeland; and we will revive our economy.

September the 11th brought out the best in America, and the best in this Congress. And I join the American people in applauding your unity and resolve. Now Americans deserve to have this same spirit directed toward addressing problems here at home. I'm a proud member of my party—yet as we act to win the war, protect our people, and create jobs in America, we must act, first and foremost, not as Republicans, not as Democrats, but as Americans.

Homeland security will make America not only stronger, but, in many ways, better.

It costs a lot to fight this war. We have spent more than a billion dollars a month—over $30 million a day—and we must be prepared for future operations. Afghanistan proved that expensive precision weapons defeat the enemy and spare innocent lives, and we need more of them. We need to replace aging aircraft and make our military more agile, to put our troops anywhere in the world quickly and safely. Our men and women in uniform deserve the best weapons, the best equipment, the best training—and they also deserve another pay raise.

My budget includes the largest increase in defense spending in two decades—because while the price of freedom and security is high, it is never too high. Whatever it costs to defend our country, we will pay.

The next priority of my budget is to do everything possible to protect our citizens and strengthen our nation against the ongoing threat of another attack. Time and distance from the events of September the 11th will not make us safer unless we act on its lessons. America is no longer protected by vast oceans. We are protected from attack only by vigorous action abroad, and increased vigilance at home.

My budget nearly doubles funding for a sustained strategy of homeland security, focused on four key areas: bioterrorism, emergency response, airport and border security, and improved intelligence. We will develop vaccines to fight anthrax and other deadly diseases. We'll increase funding to help states and communities train and equip our heroic police and firefighters. We will improve intelligence collection and sharing, expand patrols at our borders, strengthen the security of air travel, and use technology to track the arrivals and departures of visitors to the United States.

Homeland security will make America not only stronger, but, in many ways, better. Knowledge gained from bioterrorism research will improve public health. Stronger police and fire departments will mean safer neighborhoods. Stricter border enforcement will help combat illegal drugs. And as government works to better secure our homeland, America will continue to depend on the eyes and ears of alert citizens. . . .

Fighting for freedom and liberty

This time of adversity offers a unique moment of opportunity—a moment we must seize to change our culture. Through the gathering momentum of millions of acts of service and decency and kindness, I know we can overcome evil with greater good. And we have a great opportunity during this time of war to lead the world toward the values that will bring lasting peace.

All fathers and mothers, in all societies, want their children to be educated, and live free from poverty and violence. No people on Earth yearn to be oppressed, or aspire to servitude, or eagerly await the midnight knock of the secret police.

If anyone doubts this, let them look to Afghanistan, where the Islamic "street" greeted the fall of tyranny with song and celebration. Let the skeptics look to Islam's own rich history, with its centuries of learning, and tolerance and progress. America will lead by defending liberty and justice because they are right and true and unchanging for all people everywhere.

No nation owns these aspirations, and no nation is exempt from them. We have no intention of imposing our culture. But America will always stand firm for the non-negotiable demands of human dignity: the rule of law; limits on the power of the state; respect for women; private property; free speech; equal justice; and religious tolerance.

America will take the side of brave men and women who advocate these values around the world, including the Islamic world, because we have a greater objective than eliminating threats and containing resentment. We seek a just and peaceful world beyond the war on terror.

In this moment of opportunity, a common danger is erasing old rivalries. America is working with Russia and China and India, in ways we have never before, to achieve peace and prosperity. In every region, free markets and free trade and free societies are proving their power to lift lives. Together with friends and allies from Europe to Asia, and Africa to Latin America, we will demonstrate that the forces of terror cannot stop the momentum of freedom.

The last time I spoke here, I expressed the hope that life would return to normal. In some ways, it has. In others, it never will. Those of us who have lived through these challenging times have been changed by them. We've come to know truths that we will never question: evil is real, and it must be opposed. Beyond all differences of race or creed, we are one country, mourning together and facing danger together. Deep in the American character, there is honor, and it is stronger than cynicism. And many have discovered again that even in tragedy—especially in tragedy—God is near.

In a single instant, we realized that this will be a decisive decade in the history of liberty, that we've been called to a unique role in human events. Rarely has the world faced a choice more clear or consequential. Our enemies send other people's children on missions of suicide and murder. They embrace tyranny and death as a cause and a creed. We stand for a different choice, made long ago, on the day of our founding. We affirm it again today. We choose freedom and the dignity of every life. Steadfast in our purpose, we now press on. We have known freedom's price. We have shown freedom's power. And in this great conflict, my fellow Americans, we will see freedom's victory.

Thank you all. May God bless.

2

National Security Depends on the Development of Other Nations

Larry Diamond

Larry Diamond is a senior fellow at the Hoover Institution, an organization that supports private enterprise and a limited federal government.

The United States must understand and respond to the global backlash against it if the nation is to guarantee its security and win the war against terrorism. Countless people, largely from Muslim nations, blame the United States, its allies, and capitalism in general for the suffering and injustice in their own countries. However, the obstacle to development in much of the world is not capitalism but rather incompetent and corrupt governments. The United States must foster development that leads to democracy and improves the quality of life in developing nations. This foreign assistance needs to include not only money but also instruction in how to build political institutions that encourage progress.

Since [the] September 11, 2001 [terrorist attacks on America], the United States and its allies have been at war against an evil and evasive enemy. That war has vital military and operational components, which will proceed in different ways for months and probably years to come. But force alone cannot win this war. Victory requires a longer-term *political* strategy as well. We must rob the new Bolsheviks, masquerading as religious warriors, of the popular support, political sympathy, and state sponsorship they need to threaten civilized countries.

The logic of Islamic Bolsheviks

Like [Soviet leader Nikolai] Lenin himself and most of the important communist revolutionaries of the twentieth century, the leaders and strategists of the Islamic Bolsheviks are well educated and come from middle- or upper-class backgrounds. But they mobilize growing reservoirs of sympathy

From "How to Win the War," by Larry Diamond, *Hoover Digest*, no. 1, 2002. Copyright © 2002 by the Hoover Institution. Reprinted with permission.

and commitment among lower-class people who feel deprived, disempowered, and humiliated. In their time, Marxist-Leninists were able to convince broad popular followings that the causes of their suffering, and of the obvious injustices in their societies, were capitalism and imperialism.

The new Bolsheviks similarly focus their political indictment on the leading capitalist nation, the United States, and the alleged imperialism of Israel, with U.S. and Western support. And like so many communist revolutionaries of the twentieth century, they denounce numerous existing regimes—allies (however superficial) of the United States—as corrupt and exploitative. The problem for the United States is that many of the regimes we now depend on are precisely that. From Morocco to Egypt, from Saudi Arabia to Pakistan and Indonesia, predominantly Muslim populations are increasingly receptive to revolutionary and hateful appeals because they are fed up with the oppression, inequity (in most cases), poverty, and extravagant corruption in which their societies have been mired. Disgusted with their rulers, despairing of the prospect for peaceful and incremental change within the existing order, they are looking for an explanation of their personal torment and societal degradation. Like Adolf Hitler, Lenin, and other charismatic demagogues before him, Osama bin Laden offers an alluring, Manichean explanation: It is the fault of the Jews, of the international capitalist system, and of the United States and the globalizing order it is imposing.

This twisted logic is resonating emotionally among large and growing numbers of the one billion Muslims who stretch from Morocco to Indonesia—and even some who live or reside in Europe and the United States. With time, force, vigilance, and some luck, we might substantially destroy and disrupt the existing global infrastructure of terrorism. We have already achieved striking progress inside Afghanistan. But no amount of military force, law enforcement vigilance, or operational genius can contain an army of suicide bombers that stretches endlessly across borders and over time. We must ultimately undermine their capacity to recruit and indoctrinate new true believers.

Moreover, we should not assume that this new Cold War will draw its line at the boundaries of the Muslim world. Disillusionment with capitalism and democracy is mounting in much of Latin America, Asia, and the former Soviet Union. Fear and resentment of "globalization," of the democratic West—and of a United States that is portrayed as domineering and contemptuous of global sensitivities—are spreading around the world like a virus. If that virus mutates beyond its current religious boundaries—if a new antidemocratic and antiglobalist ideology takes root in Latin America, Africa, and non-Muslim parts of Eurasia—we will be in far greater danger than we already are.

Obstacles to development

It is vital to our national security that we comprehend the true causes of this global backlash and respond wisely to them. This is not—or at least not yet—a war between civilizations. It is not simply or fundamentally a clash of values or beliefs. Indeed, it stems most fundamentally from the fact that peoples around the world share some of the same goals. They want to live in dignity and prosperity. Both as individuals and as members of a group—a nation and even a religion—they want to be respected as of equal worth. Billions of people want globalization to deliver on the promise of a better life for them and their children. Most of them want freedom as well as development.

The fundamental obstacle to these aspirations is of course not capitalism or Israel or the United States. Neither is it foreign debt, the World Bank, or the legacy of colonialism or slavery. It is the venal, rotten, and incompetent governance that these peoples' rulers have visited upon them. In the Middle East and Africa, in Latin America and the former Soviet Union, and even in large parts of East Asia, no factor stands more fundamentally in the way of development, stability, and human progress than the endemic corruption of weak, unaccountable, ineffectual states. Unless this problem is addressed in a serious, aggressive, and visionary way, we are not going to win the political war on terrorism.

Ironically, even as this awful confrontation has been gathering in the past decade, we have learned a lot about what is needed to improve governance and develop societies. The challenge is to build the institutions of democracy, transparency, and participation in both the state and civil society. Sweeping reforms are needed to develop a capable, professional state bureaucracy and independent agencies that can hold government officials—the judiciary, countercorruption commissions, audit agencies, ombudsmen's commissions, economic regulatory bodies, and parliamentary oversight committees. Power must be decentralized, and local government structures must be given training and resources. Citizens need not only access to power but access to education to know their rights and the organizations to assert them in. Free and independent media must be empowered to scrutinize what government does and expose wrongdoing. Ultimately, free and fair multiparty elections are needed to further discipline government, by enabling the people to remove leaders who do not perform. If multiparty democracy is to be effective, political parties must mobilize support, engage with civil society, and seek accountability in their own structures as well as in government.

It is vital to our national security that we comprehend the true causes of this global backlash and respond wisely to them.

In many countries, it makes sense to institute competitive elections as soon as possible, both to generate incentives for reform and to provide part of the institutional means for sharing power in order to manage deadly conflicts. Where political instability is acute and democratic forces extremely weak and battered relative to extremist alternatives, however, free and fair multiparty national elections will be more viable if introduced later in a sequence of reforms to develop the structures and culture of democracy and good governance. Only such a sequence can work today in Pakistan, where the main parties and leaders of the overthrown democracy are utterly discredited.

Similarly, in Egypt and much of the Arab world, reform-minded leaders will first have to modernize the state, control corruption, build a rule of law, and open space for moderate alternatives in politics and civil society if truly competitive elections are not to lead to an Islamic fundamentalist takeover. It is true in the short run, as Lawrence Kaplan writes, that we have no alternative to these repressive regimes. But it is sheer fantasy to assume that these regimes can stagger on indefinitely through sheer repression, while their bureaucracies groan under the pressure to manufacture evermore useless jobs for exploding numbers of young people who will earn nearly worthless salaries. Unless these regimes begin to deliver real development through serious governance and market reforms, many of them are going to fall, sooner or later.

If we are serious about getting at the roots of international terrorism, . . . we must foster development that gives people hope and dignity.

Over the past two decades, through the work of institutions like the National Endowment for Democracy (NED) and the U.S. Agency for International Development (USAID), we have learned a lot about how to foster democratic and accountable governance. But political assistance is labor-intensive to manage and monitor, and it cannot be successful without adequate funding and clear coordination with our other tools of international engagement, such as diplomacy. Currently we spend about $700 million annually in democracy and governance programs in USAID, and we allocate another $30 million to NED's international grant-making program (as well as some additional funds through State Department programs). This may sound like a lot of money, until one considers that more than 100 countries in the world need assistance to improve or generate democracy and that a respectable program just to strengthen the rule of law in a medium-sized country can absorb several million dollars.

The United States' responsibility

If we are serious about getting at the roots of international terrorism, and of the spreading international sympathy it enjoys, we must foster development that gives people hope and dignity and improves the quality of their lives. In real terms, levels of U.S. development assistance have fallen dramatically since the 1970s, especially since the end of the Cold War. As Jeffrey Sachs recently observed, "The United States now spends only 0.1 percent of GNP in foreign assistance, and only 0.02 percent of GNP in assistance for the poorest countries." This is by far the weakest effort of any of the wealthy democracies.

It will not work to just throw money at the problem in some new "Marshall Plan."[1] No infusion of economic resources, no matter how massive and sustained, will in itself generate development because the problem (unlike in Europe after World War II) is not simply a lack of resources or functioning infrastructure. The problem is a more fundamental shortage of the institutions of democracy and good governance. Unless we

1. the U.S. plan to rebuild Europe's economy after World War II

help to develop countries that collect taxes, limit corruption, control crime, enforce laws, secure property rights, provide education, attract investment, and answer to their own people, countries will not develop and the violent rage against the West will not subside. Nor will we stem the proliferating threats of state collapse, international crime, drug trafficking, environmental disaster, and infectious disease, all of which breed in the swamps of economic failure and rotten governance.

This is why we must not only substantially increase our foreign assistance budget but also devote a much larger portion of that budget to democracy and governance programs, while deploying more aid workers with training in political development.

We have won an extraordinary victory in helping the people of Afghanistan free themselves from the tyranny of the Taliban. But that victory only provides us a narrow window of opportunity to begin gaining ground in a far more difficult and elusive struggle. We must help societies—in Afghanistan and around the world—build the *political* institutions that foster human progress. Only then can we achieve a lasting victory in the war on terrorism.

3

Restricting Civil Liberties During Wartime Is Justifiable

Lamar Smith

Lamar Smith, a Republican congressman from Texas, is the chair of the House Judiciary Subcommittee on Crime.

Despite the claims of the liberal media and special interest groups, the USA PATRIOT Act—legislation passed in response to the September 11, 2001, terrorist attacks on America—is not a threat to civil liberties. Although the USA PATRIOT Act does limit some liberties for several years, such restrictions are necessary during times of war to ensure national security. In addition, the provisions in the act largely enhance and update earlier legislation and are not significant shifts in policy. The act will help federal law enforcement agencies do their job more effectively and should be supported by all citizens.

The year 1984 has come and gone, and George Orwell's apocalyptic vision of the future [which he outlined in his novel *1984*] has yet to befall us. But some would have us believe that the Four Horsemen finally are upon us, and their names are [George W.] Bush, [John] Ashcroft, [Dennis] Hastert and [Trent] Lott.

If molehills really could be made into mountains, then the antiterrorism legislation, the USA PATRIOT Act, would be the most prodigious Everest of them all. Never mind that both houses of Congress and the Bush administration enacted this measure with overwhelming bipartisan support, or that the vast bulk of the American people demanded it. Since its passage into law on October 26, 2001, a small, vociferous group of the usual suspects—liberal media, ivory-tower academicians and special-interest groups—have continued to agitate against it, attempting to fan the flames of a nonexistent public hue and cry.

One of my favorite quotes by one of our most illustrious Founders is the following from Benjamin Franklin: "They that can give up essential liberty to obtain a little temporary safety deserve neither liberty nor safety:" Some might argue that Franklin was warning us against just such a day as today and just such a seemingly well-meaning piece of legislation as the antiterrorism act. However, they misread Franklin's words, as well as his intent. For the operative word in the passage is "essential."

The price of living in any society is giving up a certain degree of one's own personal liberty, and each of us does it to some extent every day. The hermit who lives alone on a mountaintop is free to wear, or not wear as the case may be, whatever he wants. He can say whatever he wants as loud as he wants. But none of us has that degree of "freedom." The price of living in a society at war is giving up a little more individual freedom and doing things differently than when living in a society at peace. Since the September 11 [terrorist attacks on America], Americans have been more restricted in where they can go and what they can do. Such has been the practice of free democracies from the golden age of Pericles in Athens to World War II.

The price of living in a society at war is giving up a little more individual freedom.

What Franklin called "essential liberty" is that core body of rights and precepts bequeathed to us by our Founding Fathers, enshrined for the most part in the Declaration of Independence, the Constitution and the Bill of Rights. They are the fundamental truths of what it means to be an American and are "the sacred rights of mankind," in the words of Alexander Hamilton, that "can never be erased or obscured by mortal power." Like our Founding Fathers before us, we must guard them jealously and never allow them to be vitiated.

The suggestion that the current legislation does so is hyperbole in the extreme. The Constitution is a sort of contract, executed by the people of the United States with the government that they created. As succeeding parties to this contract, we are inheritors not only of its rights and privileges but also its duties and obligations. Those who come to our shores never intending to become citizens—but, quite possibly, intending to cause citizens harm—never were intended to be recipients of its benefits and guarantees.

Because we believe our American system is just and right, we regularly extend the freedoms that are our birthright to other peoples, many of whom never have known freedom. Although we do so as a matter of course, it is by no means a matter of obligation. When all visitors to the United States are treated as if they, too, were fully American, then it completely nullifies what it means to be a citizen and denigrates those who aspire to such a worthy title. Simply being in America should not equal being an American.

Addressing legislative changes

Most of the provisions in the USA PATRIOT Act that have raised so much "concern" actually are directed toward foreign agents and are narrowly tailored, with additional safeguards whenever they are not. Great effort was taken to ensure that this legislation would be used on behalf of citizens of the United States, not against them.

The great genius of our system of government is that it has been able to adapt to the changes of our times. The men who worded the Constitution did so in such a way that the immutable standards they established would be just as applicable to Americans in the 21st century as in the 18th. Change is the only thing that can be counted on to stay the same, and though change is not inherently good or bad, it is necessary.

The vast bulk of the changes in the law accomplished by the USA PATRIOT Act are not substantive shifts in policy but mere revitalization of already-established precedents. "The law is like a 5-foot blanket on a 7-foot bed," it has been said. "Try as you might it'll never be able to cover everything." As soon as Congress crafts a law, outside forces—technology and basic American ingenuity—already are at work making it obsolete.

That is why [in fall 2001] federal investigators could use a search warrant to listen to a criminal's answering machine but not his voice mail. Or why it was possible to get an order to look at a suspect's e-mail but not be able to look at any of its attachments. And, even worse, because of a technicality in the 1984 Cable Act, a law-enforcement officer's warrant could be declared invalid if a terrorist's Internet service provider also was a cable company. Finally, before the USA PATRIOT Act it was commonplace to have to seek multiple warrants in multiple jurisdictions from multiple magistrates just to investigate a solitary instance of criminal activity by a single individual.

None of these results was intended or even imagined at the time the original, controlling legislation was passed. When the federal wiretap statutes were passed the rotary-dial phone was the height of telecommunications technology. The Cable Act was passed in 1984 to catch up with the cutting-edge innovation of cable television and at a time when no one had even heard of the Internet. When the laws guiding search warrants were promulgated, a single judicial district might take several days to travel across. Now one can visit several judicial districts in a single day.

The antiterrorism act has updated the anachronisms and streamlined the inconsistencies of current law. In this day and age technology changes every hour, and the criminals who use it adapt just as quickly. Because of the new changes in the law, investigators potentially now can access all of a suspect's communications without having to get 10 different wiretap orders for 10 different kinds of communications devices.

A worthy law

The final nail in the coffin's lid for the USA PATRIOT Act's opponents is the inclusion of sunset clauses. If the measures were even half as draconian as its detractors represent, then why are so many of its provisions set to expire automatically in three short years? One need not go digging through the legislation's interstices of legalese to find the answer. In fact, one needs look no further than its title. There is much to be said for a name, and the Uniting and Strengthening America by Providing Appropriate Tools Required to Intercept and Obstruct Terrorism (USA PATRIOT) Act says it all.

This legislation is not meant to be a sea change in the way civil liberties are observed in this country. It is meant to enable federal law enforcement to do its job more efficiently and effectively at a time when legal technicalities can mean the difference between life and death. Three years from now, we all presume and pray, the terrorist threat to our country will be ended. At that time, we can decide if the new laws should go or stay. In the meantime, I am comforted by my trust not only in the present administration but also in the third estate, our courts.

The USA PATRIOT Act is a law that has been debated publicly, with input and criticism from every quarter, undergoing several versions over a period of time before finally reaching its present form. It was not rushed through in the dead of the night or initiated through executive fiat by way of an executive order. It is the law of the land and worthy both of our respect and our support.

4

Civil Liberties Should Not Be Restricted During Wartime

Anthony D. Romero

Anthony D. Romero is the executive director of the American Civil Liberties Union.

Many of the provisions in the USA PATRIOT Act, which was signed into law following the September 11, 2001, terrorist attacks, pose a danger to civil liberties. The law's definition of terrorism is overly broad and could be used to criminalize legitimate and peaceful protest. Other provisions in the act could result in unlawful detention of immigrants and circumvention of the Fourth Amendment and Americans' right to privacy. In addition to the USA PATRIOT Act, other actions have been taken by the government to restrict civil liberties, including efforts to limit what the media can report. Supporters of civil liberties must remain vigilant and demand that the federal and local governments respect the Constitution.

I am very pleased to be with you today. I have long admired the City Club [a free speech forum established in 1912]. As the Citadel of Free Speech, this has become something of a hall of fame for civil libertarians.

But since I first accepted your invitation over the summer, the world and our lives have certainly been transformed.

Reminders of the September 11 tragedy and the current crisis are everywhere.

In my native New York, the markers are many and constant. You have all seen the pictures of the altered skyline; the dust and smoke in lower Manhattan, the rubble. However, what truly stands out and clutches at the heart are the faces of the thousands of "missing" people on flyers that literally wallpaper the city.

And then there are the American flags—hanging on buildings, on door stoops, on lapels, on tee shirts, on backpacks, on cars. They are literally everywhere. You see them in the hands of immigrant street hawkers, and in the windows of Arab and Sikh stores whose owners feel the need to demonstrate their solidarity with America. In many ways, the flag is the one symbol that has risen through the ash of the terrorist bombings. Showing it has become an act of defiance, an assertion that American values and American freedoms can withstand any attack.

In addition to the pride and the defiance, there have also been acts of incredible courage—by firemen, police and emergency service personnel—and acts of kindness and generosity by folks all across the country who are reaching out to help the victims and their families.

If one can talk of good news amidst such tragedy, these actions would be the topic. And there is more good news in the form of statements by President George W. Bush and many public officials, who urge all Americans to respect the rights of others and warn that attacks on Arabs and Muslims "will not stand." Although that is exactly what a U.S. President should be saying, the fact is that it has not always been the case. We know from our history that in times of national emergencies government officials have targeted particular groups for harassment or outright discrimination.

A rise in tolerance

I have asked myself why are the words of our elected officials different now, especially given the horrendous consequences of these terrible terrorist attacks? Perhaps we are more fortunate in our leaders. Perhaps we have become not only more diverse but also more tolerant and accepting of differences. Americans have often referred to their country as a "melting pot." That image assumed that all groups who reached our shores eventually assimilated into a larger body, becoming indistinguishable. The image no longer describes what is happening in our country. We now know that people do not in fact "melt" into a larger body, that many groups choose to retain their distinguishing characteristics and identities, and that, in turn, enriches our country. In that respect, we have grown more tolerant of our differences.

> *The ACLU has been in the forefront of those arguing that this is no time for Congress to be pushing through new laws that would seriously diminish our civil liberties.*

The terrorists apparently took insidious advantage of this tolerance, living in our communities and enjoying our freedoms. Does that mean that those freedoms are somehow at fault? Or that respecting the rights of others is wrong? The answer is an emphatic "No." These fundamental values, established in our Constitution, are the bedrock of our country. They are what truly distinguish us; they are the source of our unique strength; they are our legacy to the world.

I also think there is another reason for the greater measure of tolerance and respect we have witnessed so far. That is, that our message—and by "our," I refer to the American Civil Liberties Union (ACLU) and other civil liberties groups—has actually gotten through. We may be the favorite whipping post of conservative editors and the best laugh-line for late-night talk show hosts, but our efforts have not been in vain. Our defense of liberty for over 80 years has succeeded in raising people's consciousness of the Bill of Rights as something more than an appendage to the Constitution. Our efforts have kept the spotlight on these guarantees, reminding people that constitutional principles exist to be exercised, and that they are not subject to the whims of government.

The problems with the USA-Patriot Act

Which brings me to the current debate over the appropriate balance between liberty and security in a time of national crisis. After weeks of negotiation, the USA-Patriot Act was signed into law [in October 2001]. Notwithstanding the rhetoric and lip service paid to civil liberties by our nation's leaders, the new law gives government expanded power to invade our privacy, imprison people without meaningful due process, and punish dissent.

The ACLU has been in the forefront of those arguing that this is no time for Congress to be pushing through new laws that would seriously diminish our civil liberties. This is a time for reason, not hysteria. The U.S. is facing a serious threat to its security. However, that threat is directed as well to our democratic values, our freedoms, our diversity, our equality.

There are many provisions [in the USA-Patriot Act] that simply do not meet the basic test of maximizing our security and preserving our civil liberties.

There are many provisions that simply do not meet the basic test of maximizing our security and preserving our civil liberties.

I would list the following five proposals as among the most offensive:

1. The overly broad definition of "terrorism"—a definition that could easily be used against many forms of civil disobedience, including legitimate and peaceful protest. The language is so ambiguous that it is possible that if an organized group of peace demonstrators spray painted a peace sign outside of the State Department, they could be charged as terrorists for their actions.

2. Indefinite detention of immigrants based on the Attorney General's certification of a danger to national security—a harmful provision with language so vague that even the existence of judicial review would provide no meaningful safeguard against abuse.

3. Expanded wiretap authority—The new legislation minimizes judicial supervision of law enforcement wiretap authority by permitting law enforcement to obtain the equivalent of blank warrants in the physical world; authorizing intelligence wiretaps that need not specify the phone to be tapped or require that only the target's conversations be eavesdropped on. And the new law extends lower surveillance standards to the Internet.

Let me explain with regard to the Internet, since it can be rather complicated. Under current law, authorities can require a telephone company to reveal numbers dialed to and from a particular phone by simply certifying that this information is "relevant to an ongoing criminal investigation." This is far less than the probable cause standard that governs most searches and seizures. The new law extends this low level of proof to Internet communications, which, unlike a telephone number, reveal personal and private information, such as which Internet sites an individual has visited. Once that lower standard is applied to the Internet, law enforcement officers would have unprecedented power to monitor what citizens do on the Net, thereby opening a "back door" on the content of personal communications.

4. The use of "sneak and peek" searches to circumvent the Fourth Amendment—Under this segment of the legislation, law enforcement officials could enter your home, office or other private place and conduct a search, take photographs and download your computer files without notifying you until after the fact. This delayed notice provision undercuts the spirit of the Fourth Amendment and the need to provide information to citizens when their privacy is invaded by law enforcement authorities.

5. Eviscerating the wall between foreign surveillance and domestic criminal investigation—The new legislation gives the Director of Central Intelligence the power to manage the gathering of intelligence in America and mandate the disclosure of information obtained by the FBI about terrorism in general—even if it is about law-abiding American citizens—to the CIA.

These are just the "top five" problems with the proposed legislation. There are others that are equally troubling. Technology, in particular, presents problems for safeguarding security and liberty. Terrorists, on the one hand, can use it to evade conventional surveillance. On the other hand, the government has sophisticated technology that is capable of spreading a broad surveillance net that captures the communications of ordinary citizens as well as suspected criminals. That's why a sunset measure on the wiretapping proposals is the one piece of good news. It allows us the opportunity to take another look at these measures when tempers have cooled.

Learning from history

Unfortunately, the debate in Congress over changes in law enforcement powers has drawn attention away from more salient questions—questions that should have preceded the rush to advance new laws. Namely, how did September 11 evade our intelligence services? What powers do law enforcement agencies now have? And, how can these existing powers be used more effectively to combat terrorism?

In enacting laws, we must tread cautiously, but we must also stand by our principles. I say this because American history teaches us that we have tended to move in the wrong direction in times of national emergency.

In fact, our history teaches us three valuable lessons:

1. Conscription of opinion often goes hand in hand with conscription of soldiers. During World War I, soldiers were not the only ones conscripted; public opinion and the First Amendment were also conscripted as the government attempted to squelch free expression and dissent. Even good civil libertarians, swept up by the patriotic fervor, offered elaborate ra-

tionalizations for the war effort, including the suppression of free speech. Similar actions were taken during World War II, and the ACLU, in particular, was the target of popular criticism. In April 1939, the Board of Directors answered such criticism in a public statement. They said: "When the rights of any are sacrificed, the rights of none are safe."

American history teaches us that we have tended to move in the wrong direction in times of national emergency.

Sadly, we are finding similar efforts to conscript the First Amendment in service of the "war against terrorism." ACLU offices across the country have begun receiving complaints of efforts to limit free speech. In colleges and universities, we are hearing of efforts to limit academic freedom and quell dissent and debate.

And on October 11, 2001, we saw troubling efforts to conscript public opinion when the White House requested that broadcast media outlets edit or decline to show any video tapes of Osama bin Laden. No evidence of secret messages or coding was provided in the White House request, and in any case, the tapes were broadcast worldwide and were available on-line. Yet, the White House endeavored to conscript public opinion and information in the name of the war against terrorism.

The free exchange of ideas, open debate and peaceful dissent are even more important during periods of national crisis.

Violations of civil liberties

2. National crises tend to encourage gross violations of due process. Following World War I, strikes in our nation's cities terrified millions of Americans who saw law and order collapsing. In 1918, riots broke out, paralyzing the country, and federal troops were called to restore order in many cities. In June of that year, the country was shaken by a series of politically motivated bombings, including an explosion at the home of Attorney General A. Mitchell Palmer.

What ensued was one of the worst violations of civil liberties in American history. During raids in November and January, law enforcement officials swooped down on suspected radicals in 33 cities, arresting 6,000 people, most of them immigrants. The raids involved wholesale abuses of the law: arrests without a warrant, unreasonable searches and seizures, wanton destruction of property, physical brutality, and prolonged detention.

While the initial reaction to the raids was favorable, the tide of public opinion soon changed. Prominent lawyers like Felix Frankfurter raised concerns that the abuses "struck at the foundation of American free institutions, and brought the name of our country into disrepute." The Palmer Raids, as they were known, also sparked another response—the founding of the American Civil Liberties Union by Roger Baldwin and a handful of other friends. We were born out of that national crisis, to fight the good fight in this one.

Today, government officials have refused to reassure the American people that the Palmer Raids are no more than a disappointing chapter in our history books. They have refused to reassure the American people that our constitutional protections are in place, and that due process of law is alive and well. The ACLU [has] joined a coalition of civil liberties, human rights and public interest organizations in filing a freedom of information act request about the 1,000 individuals arrested or detained since September. We were compelled to file this request, because the government refused to answer our previous inquiries about the individuals in detention, whether they had access to counsel and family members, and the status of the charges against them. The courts may be our only avenue for ensuring that due process of law is a reality during coming months of this crisis.

Defending liberty during a time of national crisis is the ultimate act of defiance.

---

3. Our national leaders will often exploit popular fear of foreigners during crisis periods. Theodore Roosevelt, speaking in World War I, warned that the "Hun within our gates is the worst of the foes of our own household." His comment reflected the xenophobic sentiment in our country that led to racial profiling and ethnic bashing aimed against Germans, Italians, Jews and people from Eastern Europe.

But the most traumatic example of allowing national crises to fuel the fires of xenophobia was to be found in World War II, when the government evacuated more than 120,000 Japanese-Americans from the West Coast and held them in internment camps.

In March of 1942, the ACLU protested President Franklin Roosevelt's action. Although the ACLU lost that battle in 1942, the government eventually acknowledged its wrongful actions and in 1989 paid restitution to Japanese internees.

Liberty must be defended

For these reasons, we must resist the temptation to over-react, to rush to judgment. Cooler heads need to prevail if we are to defend our country and our liberty. The attack of September 11 not only targeted our personal lives and property, it was also an attack on the freedom and equality that are the hallmarks of our democracy.

Terror, by its very nature, is intended not only to destroy, but also to intimidate a people, forcing them to take actions that are not in their best interest.

That's why defending liberty during a time of national crisis is the ultimate act of defiance. It is the ultimate act of patriotism. For, if we are intimidated to the point of restricting our freedoms, the terrorists will have won.

Security and liberty do not have to be at odds, nor put on a collision course. We must take action to defend against any assault on civil liberties. However, we should be prepared not only to react, but also to be proactive, offering alternative solutions where feasible.

So what do we do? A proactive agenda has several parts:

First, we need to urge our fellow Americans to think carefully and clearly about the tradeoffs between national security and individual freedom, and to understand that some will seek to restrict freedom for ideological and other reasons that have little to do with security.

Second, we need to stay informed and involved in the current congressional deliberations over anti-terror legislation. We have to let our elected officials know that our eyes are on them. We have to remain vigilant not just in Washington, but in state capitals and city councils since elected officials are also attempting to pass new security legislation at the state and local levels.

Third, we must demand that government take the necessary efforts to prevent and punish unwarranted, bigoted attacks on fellow citizens of Arab descent and members of religious minorities, including Muslims and Sikhs. The Arab American Institute has documented over 300 anti-Arab incidents in the U.S. There are roughly 6.5 million Muslims, 3.5 million Arab Americans, and half a million Sikhs residing in the U.S. They are our neighbors, friends, co-workers, not the enemy.

We need to urge our fellow Americans to think carefully and clearly about the tradeoffs between national security and individual freedom.

As Arab Americans, Muslims and Sikhs continue to experience bias attacks, racial profiling and unfair treatment, the law must offer shelter to the vulnerable segments of our communities.

Fourth, we must keep the pressure on other issues. We do not have the luxury of putting other civil liberties on the backburner. We must not lose the momentum on important struggles like the death penalty or electoral reform. The tide was with us prior to September 11 and we must keep the pressure on.

Fifth, we must demand government accountability and responsiveness to civil liberties. The American people have a right to know that our basic protections are in place. Our government officials—including [attorney general] Mr. [John] Ashcroft and [FBI director] Mr. [Robert] Mueller—took oaths to uphold the U.S. Constitution. Those oaths were taken in public—not in secret. And the American people must be reassured in public that due process is alive and well. And if our constitutional protections are not secure, the ACLU will do what we do best. We'll sue.

Finally, we should establish guidelines for evaluating new proposals that would affect our basic civil liberties. At the very least, proposed changes to restrict liberty should be examined and debated in public; they should be proven effective in increasing safety and security; and they should be fairly applied in a non-discriminatory manner.

The American people must be reassured that constitutional guarantees will apply in times of crisis and tranquility alike.

I want to close with the words of a former ACLU Board member that seem especially appropriate in the current context. The Board member was Thurgood Marshall, who in a 1972 Supreme Court opinion wrote:

"This is a country which stands tallest in troubled times, a country that clings to fundamental principles, cherishes its constitutional heritage, and rejects simple solutions that compromise the values that lie at the roots of our democratic system."

Next time you see a flag on a building, door or lapel, think of Justice Marshall's words. And remember that history will surely judge our patriotism by our steadfast commitment to the principles of liberty and freedom that are the heart and soul of the flag. So let's wave it proudly.

Thank you very much.

5

Immigration Control Must Be Strengthened to Protect Against Terrorism

David Simcox

David Simcox is chair of the policy board of the Center for Immigration Studies, an organization that supports immigration policies that are both pro-immigrant and low-immigration.

The attacks of September 11, 2001, prove that it is too easy for foreign terrorists to enter the United States. Consequently, Congress must take steps to strengthen immigration control, thereby improving national security. Politicians should stop resisting the development of a national ID card. Congress should also work with government agencies and professional organizations to ensure that birth and death certificates and other vital records are secure and accurate. Most importantly, the federal government needs to track the entrances and departures of foreigners, in particular those who enter with work or student visas. However, Congress has been ambivalent about developing tracking systems. Regardless which steps are taken to control immigration, such efforts must take place as soon as possible.

America's political leaders have never seen much political opportunity in laws controlling and monitoring the political behavior of aliens in the United States. The nation suffers from a two-century old "Alien and Sedition Act hangover." The outer limits of individual freedom, privacy, and civil rights have steadily expanded in the popular mind since the Vietnam era, along with a willingness to extend these values to aliens just joining or seeking to join our society. The beatific vision of an "inclusionary society" has at times edged out ordinary prudence. Rising anti-regulatory instincts, coupled with the tight labor market of the middle and late 1990s, reinforced the aversions of opinion and business leaders to controls, nearly nullifying employer sanctions legislation.

Excerpted from "Identifying, Screening, and Tracking Aliens," by David Simcox, *Social Contract*, Fall 2000. Copyright © 2000 by The Social Contract Press. Reprinted with permission.

A record of weak control

September 11, 2001, should have been the shrillest and most imperious alarm bell of all. A solid eighty percent of those polled by CBS-*New York Times* immediately after the trade center bombings agreed that it is too easy for foreigners to enter the U.S. Of the nineteen known hijackers, fifteen entered with visas through legal ports of entry, though a number overstayed. Some were admitted despite being flagged somewhere in federal lookout databases. Several entered on stolen passports. Most easily acquired drivers licenses even though out of status and misrepresenting their identities. And some detainees acquired the more carefully screened Commercial Driver's License, allowing them to drive hazardous material trucks. The extent of the terrorist groups' illegal presence in the U.S. is apparent in the more than one hundred suspects and possible material witnesses that the Immigration and Naturalization Service (INS) has been able to hold on immigration violations.

> *Will September 11 awaken Congress and the public to the essentiality of immigration controls to national security and tranquility?*

The record of immigration control during the last decade and a half shows a pattern of Congressional willingness to adopt mildly restrictive legislation and then either weaken it with provisos and amendments, delay implementation, or fail to provide the funds and political backing to carry it through. Will September 11 awaken Congress and the public to the essentiality of immigration controls to national security and tranquility? Or will they resume business as usual as they did after the 1996 legislative efforts?

This moment of public alarm and shifting perceptions in an endangered nation calls for an assessment of major immigration ID and tracking systems—existing or proposed—to determine how they might be strengthened to meet the threat, put into place more quickly, or moved forward from the recommendation stage.

The national ID debate

Fully seventy percent of respondents told Pew Research Center pollsters following the New York terror that they would favor a national ID card to be carried at all times and shown to police on request. While this is somewhat higher than before September 11, previous polls in the 1990s have regularly shown a solid majority favors national ID.

But in Congress the term "national ID card" is regularly used as a lethal epithet against most measures to improve national identification. Probably the most important casualty of this psychosis was the 1996 law mandating the recording of drivers license applicants' social security numbers and their verification by the Social Security Administration (SSA). Labeled as an effort to "federalize" the state driver's license and "create a national ID card," the provision was first delayed then rescinded by hostile lawmakers.

Illustrating our off-again on-again approach toward better ID is Congress's recent effort (H.R. 4857) to forbid states to use the social security number at all in drivers' licenses or their accompanying databases. The more than twenty states now using the social security number in licensing would be required to cease by 2003.

The irony is inescapable. Those who opposed higher security standards for drivers' licenses by arguing state prerogatives have ended up denying states the right to set their own license security standards. The legislation also proposes other measures to restrict federal, state, and local agencies' use of the social security number. To its credit, Congress did enact legislation (S. 2924) in 2000 that bans the Internet sale of false driver's licenses and other ID documents. The law closes a loophole that has allowed Internet purveyors of counterfeit documents to claim that they are sold for "novelty or entertainment purposes only." At this point, upgrading and verifying our de facto national ID, the driver's license, is the most readily available and practical option for promptly developing a uniform, secure ID.

The Social Security Administration (SSA) in 1997 fulfilled its 1996 legislative mandate to present the options for making the social security card a counterfeit-resistant, tamperproof, biometric-based national identification document. SSA's 1997 study presented seven plausible options varying in their degree of technological wizardry. The costs SSA estimated for equipping nearly 300 million Americans and residents with the card ranged from $3.9 billion to $7.3 billion. The concept remains just that, a concept. Neither the Bush Administration nor SSA so far have indicated interest in following up on it and Congress, in H.R. 4857, has seemed more interested in restricting the use of the social security number as an identification tool.

Securing vital records

A reliable national identification system (which would not necessarily involve a card) remains a pipe dream in the absence of more reliable and secure government breeder documents. Here, as elsewhere, progress to improve the integrity and uniformity of vital records has been spotty, notwithstanding explicit direction in the 1996 immigration reforms. Section 656 of the Illegal Immigration Reform and Immigrant Responsibility Act (IIRIRA) and various amendments designated INS as the lead agency in a federal-state working group to develop and issue regulations setting security standards birth certificates must meet for acceptance by federal agencies.

The act also tasked the Department of Health and Human Services (HHS) to work with the states, using grants, to develop a system for matching birth and death records and rapid (electronic) reporting of deaths. SSA, no longer in the HHS, has made more progress than INS, though both lag far behind the time frame envisaged by legislators. State vital statistics agencies, and their professional association in Washington, with a grant from SSA, are well along on a pilot for electronic reporting of deaths. A pilot for electronic reporting of births is in the planning stage. INS, however, and its collaborating state and federal agencies, are still far from setting federal standards on birth certificates.

Most of the progress toward more secure vital records in the late 1990s is due to the work of the state vital records and motor vehicle agencies and their professional associations, the National Association of Public Health Statistics and Information Systems (NAPHSIS) and the American Association of Motor Vehicle Administrators (AAMVA). NAPHSIS and its member agencies have cooperated with the State Department on systematizing verification of suspect birth certificates of passport applicants. AAMVA has been working since 1994 to establish a model program for uniform identification practices for state agencies to help them to combat fraud. Among their goals: To see each state's MVA linked electronically with SSA, INS, and vital record agencies for rapid exchange of information on individuals and documents. AAMVA shares the general view among professionals in the field that document fraud cannot be effectively curbed until there is electronic verification.

Despite continued difficulty with applying computerized information systems, the INS has made considerable progress in modernizing and securing its own alien ID and data systems. In the past decade, the agency has adopted tamper-resistant Permanent Resident (green) cards and employment authorization cards. Both now have expiration dates. INS and the State Department instituted a combination tourist visa/border crossing card, using laser technology. INS has also invested heavily in forensic research and scrutiny on questionable documents, and more training of government and private sector document inspectors to recognize fraud. INS's and the State Department's emphasis on machine-readability of ID documents improves databases and watch lists with their rapid and accurate capture of high volumes of individual case data.

Nothing could be more basic for a modern state than knowing who is within its boundaries.

In the past decade INS has installed IDENT, an automated fingerprint identification system (AFIS), to collect data on captured illegal aliens. The system is promising. It was not technical failure but lack of staff training that caused INS's embarrassing failure to recognize and hold fugitive Mexican serial killer Maturino Resendiz in June 1999. An unamused Congress ordered a five-year project to combine IDENT with the FBI's fingerprint identification system.

National security considerations

SSA and the states are moving haltingly in the direction of higher standards for breeder documents as envisaged in the 1996 act. Problems are lack of money and staff, privacy objections, local politics, revenue issues and, more recently, legislative moves to limit use of the social security number.

• Public pressure is needed to get greater urgency into these projects and, particularly, to move INS to produce timely rules on tighter federal birth certificate standards.

• The attempts of Congress to restrict state use of the SSN for drivers' licenses must be resisted.

• *More federal incentives and support are needed for the smaller states to match birth and death records and improve the security of those records.*
• *Federal-state agency networks for electronic verification of INS and State Department documents and state-issued documents are a must.* . . .

Developing tracking systems

Nothing could be more basic for a modern state than knowing who is within its boundaries, particularly those who are not citizens. But the U.S. has rarely been comfortable exercising this faculty. The Attorney General ended the mandatory annual registration of alien residents in the late 1970s. Illegal aliens have surreptitiously settled here by the millions in the last three decades. At least forty percent of the settled illegal alien population of six to eight million did not sneak in to the country, but entered originally documented as temporary visitors. Some thirty million foreigners now enter yearly with temporary authorization, but there has been no process for determining if they leave, and in the case of those who come to study or work, no way of knowing whether they are doing what they came to do or where they are doing it.

The built-in tendency to treat immigration as a marginal security interest must be resisted.

A visa waiver authority for citizens of twenty-nine countries deemed to be low-risk for overstaying now allows seventeen million persons a year—more than half of all temporary entrants—to come in for up to ninety days without being vetted at all by U.S. consuls abroad. Legislation in 2000 made the waiver program a permanent feature of immigration law. The U.S. requires only that the waiver country give reciprocity and adopt a machine-readable passport. The waiver country's citizens forfeit the right to certain legal remedies to remain in the U.S., and of course must be from a country that at one time had a refusal rate on visa application in U.S. Consular posts of three percent or less. The increasing use of machine-readable passports eases INS's task of capturing a record of entry—though a number of visa waiver countries will not have passports that meet U.S. standards until as late as 2007. But whether or when those using this privilege actually depart the U.S. is largely unknown.

The waiver allows the State Department to save on visa officer positions, but the Justice Department is less enthusiastic about it. The procedure increases the time demands on its inspection staff at U.S. ports of entry. A further, growing problem is that the waiver increases the value of waiver country passports to prospective illegal entrants, criminals, and terrorists. Counterfeiting of visa waiver passports has flourished in frequency and sophistication.

Section 110 of the 1996 IIRIRA aims at documenting the departures of temporary visitors. The provision directed the Attorney General to develop within two years an automated entry and exit control system for collecting a departure record of every alien and matching it with an arrival record to identify visa overstayers.

The plan's subsequent fate is an example of Congress's ambivalence on tracking systems. Following its adoption, and reacting to the anger of U.S. border-area business interests, a coalition of border state legislators led by then Senate immigration subcommittee chairman Spencer Abraham of Michigan worked to delay implementation of the project and, later, change it from an action program to a pilot. Since snarled land border traffic to and from Canada was the dominant concern, INS was allowed to proceed with improving ongoing collection of departure records at air and seaports, where departing aliens are already required to surrender their I-94 entry forms (but often do not). The Clinton administration and INS itself showed little enthusiasm for pressing ahead with the system as originally enacted because of its size and scope and drain on manpower.

Five years after the passage of Section 110, immigration officials are authorized to verify departures of only a fraction of visiting aliens. Congress's latest reenactment of Section 110 (Public Law 106-215) in June, 2000, still showed no urgency in getting a system up and working. The latest law authorizes an "Integrated Entry and Exit Data System" to be in operation by the end of 2003 for the 210 air and seaports of entry, the end of 2004 for fifty of the 190 land ports of entry, and the end of 2005 for all 400 full service ports of entry. Congress insisted that the systems chosen must rely on existing data sources. It is uncertain how the Secretary of State and the Attorney General can develop effective systems at land ports of entry in the face of the law's explicit denial of authority to ". . . impose any new documentary or data collection requirements on any person."

National security considerations

• *Washington would be justified in revisiting Section 110 to advance the effective dates at all categories of ports of entry and permit reasonable additional data collection.*

• *The visa refusal rate is an insufficient measure of a nation's suitability for a visa waiver. The visa waiver law provides for emergency revocation of the privilege to any country. This authority should be applied against countries whose passports show more than a minimal propensity to forgery or alteration.*

• *Revocation of the waiver should be mandatory for countries that the new entry-exit verification systems show have more than a negligible overstay rate. Reviews of country overstay rates should be made now using available INS information on sea and air departures.*

• *To aid data collection, the government should consider closing smaller ports of entry and exit and require that all overland entry and departures by non-NAFTA temporary entrants be limited to selected border crossing points.*

Monitoring foreign students and temporary workers

Steven Emerson, an expert on terrorism, warned Congress in 2000 that at least two hundred terrorists' agents received student visas in the 1990s and have pursued graduate or undergraduate training here. It is now known that some of the terrorist pilots of September 11 received their training at U.S. aviation schools with technical training (M) visas. Emerson noted that terrorists and militants have used university student (F) or cultural exchange (J) visas to enter the U.S. for shorter periods, often with invitations to religion-based conferences and meetings of Islamic organizations. But their true mission is to recruit activists, raise funds, coordinate strategies, indoctrinate U.S. Moslems, and even in some cases train in terrorist tactics. Many are able to get the visas with false identification or by omission from or inadequate checking of U.S. watch lists.

A 1998 report of the federal Commission to Assess the Ballistic Missile Threat to the United States stated that the "acquisition and use of transferred technologies in ballistic missiles and weapons of mass destruction has been facilitated by foreign students training in the U.S." FBI Director Louis Freeh warned Congress in 1996 that "some foreign governments task foreign students specifically to acquire information of a variety of technical subjects. . . And on completion of their studies are encouraged to seek employment with U.S. firms to steal proprietary information." FBI chief of anti-terrorism Dale Watson in 1998 cited Iran as a country whose government relies heavily on students in the United States for low-level intelligence and technical expertise. Senator Diane Feinstein, who serves on the Senate's subcommittee on terrorism, has noted that between 1991 and 1996 the State Department issued 10,000 student visas to nationals of Iran, Iraq, Syria, Sudan, and Libya, all cited by the State Department as sponsors of terrorism.

Given the euphoria of opinion leaders about immigration, and resistance from the universities and colleges, the proposal to create a system to track foreign students has lagged badly since its enactment in 1996. The law directed Justice, State, and Education to work together on a system to electronically collect information from educational institutions on the identity, address, academic status, and disciplinary actions of foreign students holding F, J, and M category visas from five countries. This phase was to be completed by January 1, 1998, and was to be financed by fees, paid by the foreign students, now set at $95 a year. A serious sticking point has been the refusal of colleges and universities to collect the fees. The INS will now do it. The full program will begin with the spring semester of 2002 and will apply only to students enrolled since 1999. Originally known by the acronym CIPRIS (Coordinated Interagency Partnership Regulating International Students), the system was renamed SEVIS this year (Student and Exchange Visitor Information System).

National security considerations

Except for its four-year delay in implementation, SEVIS is an innovative and promising system for monitoring a particularly mercurial group of long-term, overstay-prone foreign visitors and holding the universities who recruit them more accountable for ensuring their compliance with long-neglected student visa law and regulations. It also adheres to the growing conviction in Washington that immigrants, whether visitor or temporary, should pay much more of the cost of the services and oversight they receive.

• The downside of the program is its refusal to address the sizable numbers of foreign students who enrolled before 1999, many of whom have fallen into irregular status. This limitation should be dropped.

• The successful testing and startup of SEVIS provides an opportunity to extend the system, or a similar one, to other temporary worker, student, or re-

searcher categories that impinge on national security or the high tech economy and labor force. Long-term temporary categories that merit similar reporting and tracking, most of which are sponsored or hosted by U.S.-based institutions, would be treaty traders (E), professional and technical workers (H), journalists (I), intracompany transferees (L), and (R) religious workers.

• *Bring the Departments of Defense and Energy into the interagency group running SEVIS to improve assessments of the transfer of sensitive technology through foreign graduate students.*

• *Suspend issuance of all student visas for one year and reduce the number of schools eligible to enroll foreign students, eliminating immigration and diploma mills and marginal vocational and technical schools.*

Avoid massive programs

The terrorist threat will not wait for languorous interagency studies and pilot projects. Speed is vital. Those systems already up and running must be put to full use. Those successfully tested must be installed rapidly. Resources will inevitably be a major consideration.

• The built-in tendency to treat immigration as a marginal security interest must be resisted, as should the temptation to draw on INS resources, such as Border Patrol officers, to more spectacular, but not necessarily more vital, duties.

• The INS cannot afford more disruption at this critical point. Plans for massive reorganization of the agency should be held in abeyance. Political leaders particularly should avoid imposing vast new immigration and naturalization benefit programs—such as amnesties, guest worker intakes, and broad humanitarian projects—that would divert the staffs of INS and the State Department from security and enforcement projects.

• The most efficient way of monitoring prospective terrorists is to deny them entry in the first place. INS should get the funds and people to open pre-inspection stations at additional major foreign airports and to supplement the work of U.S. officers in posts of high visa demand.

6

Immigrants Are Not Being Treated Fairly in America's War Against Terrorism

Jeffrey Rosen

Jeffrey Rosen is the legal affairs editor at the New Republic.

In the wake of the September 11, 2001, terrorist attacks, Attorney General John Ashcroft has authorized the detention and deportation of more than a thousand noncitizens who are suspected of having ties to terrorism. Although these detentions are not unconstitutional, Ashcroft's policy is appalling and will not strengthen national security. Detained immigrants are denied important rights, such as access to appointed counsel and lawyer-client privilege. Earlier decisions by the Supreme Court suggest that the judicial system will not protect immigrants from mistreatment, so it is up to Congress to guarantee the rights of detained aliens.

O f all the new security measures adopted by the [George W.] Bush administration since September 11, 2001, the most draconian involve the detention and interrogation of aliens. In his dragnet effort to uncover evidence of terrorism, Attorney General John Ashcroft has authorized the detention of some 1,100 noncitizens. Some have been held for months and—thanks to recently passed legislation—may be held indefinitely. Critics call the Ashcroft detentions unconstitutional. "We have violated core constitutional principles," says David Cole of Georgetown University Law Center, pointing to new laws and regulations that allow the government to detain aliens without bail; deport or exclude them because of their political associations; and eavesdrop on their conversations with their attorneys.

Some of these measures may indeed violate principles of procedural fairness, free speech, and privacy. But they don't violate the Constitution. Over the last 50 years the Supreme Court has imposed few constitutional restraints on the ability of Congress and the president to detain, exclude,

From "Holding Pattern," by Jeffrey Rosen, *New Republic*, December 10, 2001. Copyright © 2001 by *New Republic*. Reprinted with permission.

and deport aliens in ways that would be grossly unconstitutional if applied to citizens. As a result, Ashcroft has virtually unlimited legal discretion in his treatment of aliens. But that doesn't mean he shouldn't be stopped, only that judges aren't the people to stop him. Although it may be difficult in the current environment, our elected representatives in Congress are the only officials authorized to determine the fate and defend the interests of mistreated aliens. It's a role Congress has been reluctant to play in the past. But Congress may be the only hope we've got.

Detaining aliens

The most sweeping of the laws and regulations passed in the wake of September 11 are those that authorize the indefinite detention of aliens whom Ashcroft designates as suspected terrorists. Most significantly, on November 14, 2001, the Immigration and Naturalization Service (INS) adopted a regulation allowing the detention of aliens whom the government wants to deport but no other country will admit. If the attorney general, in consultation with the State Department, believes that their cases raise significant "national security or terrorism concerns," the aliens can be locked up indefinitely.

The regulation is an attempt to respond to the *Zadvydas* case, decided by the Supreme Court [in June 2001]. Before then, the Court had repeatedly held that Congress has virtually unlimited power to deport, exclude, or detain immigrants at the border. In *Zadvydas,* however, Justice Stephen Breyer, writing for the 5-4 majority, held that in the 1996 immigration reform act, Congress hadn't intended to authorize the indefinite detention of aliens who couldn't be deported because their home countries wouldn't allow them back. (In fact, Congress probably had intended to authorize the detentions; Breyer stretched the language of the law to avoid a constitutional conflict.) But even though Breyer intervened on behalf of aliens' rights, his opinion included an important loophole: It stressed that Congress and the president might have more leeway to detain aliens indefinitely in cases involving "terrorism or other special circumstances where special arguments might be made for forms of preventative detention and for heightened deference to the judgments of the political branches with respect to matters of national security."

Our elected representatives in Congress are the only officials authorized to determine the fate and defend the interests of mistreated aliens.

The new INS regulations exploit this loophole for all it's worth. They allow John Ashcroft and [Secretary of State] Colin Powell unilaterally to detain any deportable alien whose release would have "serious adverse foreign policy consequences," in the government's opinion. And although the regulations give the government tremendous discretion to define a foreign policy crisis, it's hard to imagine that the Supreme Court would raise constitutional objections. This is particularly true in light of the USA Patriot Act, passed in October 2001, in which Congress explicitly authorized the attorney general to detain "suspected terrorists" indefinitely in special circumstances. This time, there's no ambiguity about congressional intent.

Another element of the USA Patriot Act allows the deportation not only of convicted terrorists, but of any alien who provides financial support to a "terrorist organization," broadly defined as a group of people who threaten to use weapons. "I would guess that somebody who writes a check to the organizations that raise money for the IRA (Irish Republican Army) might be brought within this," says Peter Schuck of Yale Law School. "That's troubling, but it's hard to see how it could be more precisely defined." Schuck suggests that judges might interpret the law to say that the IRA contributor can't be convicted as a terrorist unless he knows more about how the IRA operates than it takes to write a check. But once again, it's a mistake to rely on the courts: In the past, the Supreme Court has been extremely deferential to Congress in cases involving the deportation of unpopular aliens.

In the 1950s, for example, Congress passed the McCarran-Walter Act, which allowed the government to exclude and deport aliens who advocated communism. The Supreme Court upheld the attorney general's right to deport aliens who were members of the Communist Party, suggesting that Congress has the right to treat aliens in ways that would violate the First Amendment if applied to citizens. The Court held that an alien couldn't use his lack of knowledge about the Communist Party's goals as a defense. It also held that aliens could be detained without bail while the government decided what to do with them. These cold war precedents may doom any legal challenges to a regulation issued by the INS in October 2001 allowing the Justice Department to lock up aliens while appealing an immigration judge's decision to release them on bail.

Further restrictions for aliens

The Patriot Act also authorizes Congress to exclude from the United States any aliens who "endorse or espouse terrorist activity" or who "persuade others to support terrorist activity or a terrorist organization." In 1953 the Supreme Court upheld similar exclusions. In a famous case, a Romanian alien named Mezei, who had lived in the United States for 25 years, went home to visit his dying mother; when he tried to return, he was detained on Ellis Island for almost two years on grounds that his admission would be "prejudicial to the public interest." The Supreme Court held that he wasn't even entitled to judicial review of the decision not to release him on bail. Harry Kalven, the great First Amendment scholar at the University of Chicago, summed up the Court's attitude toward exclusion and deportation of suspected Communists this way: "The rule was that there were absolutely no limits on the power of Congress to exclude aliens. Neither inhibitions against gross racial discrimination, against interference with freedom of speech and association, against breaking up the family, nor restraints dictated by notions of basic procedural fairness could stay the hand of the government."

All this would be easier to swallow if the government had to prove that the aliens it was indefinitely locking up really did threaten national security. Unfortunately, because deportation hearings are considered civil—not criminal—proceedings, immigrants have none of the rights available in criminal trials: to appointed counsel, to the exclusion of illegally seized evidence, to have the government prove their dangerousness beyond reasonable doubt.

> *The Ashcroft rule isn't only an egregious incursion on privacy—it will also bring little in the way of increased security.*

A detained alien does have the right to a lawyer—if he can afford one. But in his most appalling decision of all, Ashcroft has undermined this right as well. On October 30, 2001, the attorney general approved a rule allowing federal agents to eavesdrop on conversations between federal inmates and their lawyers whenever "reasonable suspicion exists to believe that an inmate may use the communications with attorneys . . . to facilitate acts of terrorism." Even though an inmate's conversation with his lawyer can't be used against him by a criminal prosecutor, the presence of federal monitors will severely inhibit the ability of detainees—innocent as well as guilty—to speak candidly with their lawyers and receive necessary legal advice.

The Ashcroft rule isn't only an egregious incursion on privacy—it will also bring little in the way of increased security. After all, lawyers already can't help their clients commit new crimes, and they have an ethical obligation to report threats of terrorism or violence. Under the so-called "crime/fraud exception" to the attorney-client privilege, if the government has probable cause to believe that a client is using a lawyer to advance an illegal scheme, it can get a court order or even set up a sting operation. Moreover, as Akhil Reed Amar of Yale Law School suggests, there are less-intrusive ways of ensuring that the most dangerous suspects don't use their lawyers to further terrorist schemes: Lawyer-client conversations could be videotaped and reviewed by impartial judges, for example, rather than by partisan government lawyers. But although the Ashcroft eavesdropping scheme is unnecessary and indefensible, it doesn't violate the right to counsel. The Sixth Amendment protects the attorney-client privilege only in a criminal prosecution, while most of the aliens who will have their conversations spied on by John Ashcroft will never be charged with a crime.

Congress must respond

If the courts won't protect aliens from John Ashcroft, who can? The answer, for better or worse, is Congress. The Bush administration has shown little restraint in the domestic war against terrorism. And like any risk-averse federal agency, the INS is resorting to dragnets to protect itself against the charges of negligence that will inevitably follow if more aliens commit terrorist acts. As Schuck suggests, Congress should carefully oversee the Justice Department's enforcement of the new laws and regulations authorizing the detention of aliens. The Constitution, after all, gives Congress, rather than the president, plenary authority over immigration. One of the many unfortunate features of Ashcroft's decision to permit eavesdropping on attorney-client conversations is that it was announced without consulting Congress. Vermont Senator Pat Leahy is sufficiently exercised by Ashcroft's failure to consult Congress on a range of issues, including the establishment of military courts, that he has scheduled oversight hearings. If Congress remains jealous of its prerogatives to determine the fate of aliens, perhaps its oversight will restrain an administration unwilling to restrain itself.

Unfortunately, history does not offer much cause for optimism. "The communist deportation cases supply almost experiment evidence of how little Congress itself is disciplined by the traditions of political tolerance," wrote Harry Kalven. "They suggest that Congress, when freed from constitutional restraints, will pursue the logic of security relentlessly."

In an even more famous abdication, Congress failed to object to the detention of Japanese-Americans during World War II. It took 43 years for Congress to recognize its error. The Civil Liberties Act of 1988 issued an apology and $20,000 to each of the Japanese-American citizens and resident aliens interned during World War II. "We know we're going to regret this," says Alex Aleinikoff, a former general counsel of the INS under President Clinton. "Probably now is the time we should be saying to the detained aliens, 'We know we're taking something from you and we should pay you later.'" Better yet, of course, would be not to detain them unreasonably in the first place.

7

Military Commissions Should Be Used to Prosecute Terrorists

Abraham D. Sofaer and Paul R. Williams

Abraham D. Sofaer is a senior fellow at the Hoover Institution, which supports private enterprise and limited federal government, and a law professor at Stanford University in Palo Alto, California. Paul R. Williams is an assistant professor of law and international relations at American University in Washington, D.C.

Military commissions, not the American domestic court system, are the preferred way of prosecuting accused terrorists. The American domestic criminal justice system is not designed to fight terrorism or prosecute war crimes. In comparison, military commissions are specifically intended for situations in which suspected terrorists are in the custody of the American government. These commissions, which should build upon the military tribunals used in Yugoslavia, are fair, flexible, and can protect sensitive information.

On November 13, 2001, President George W. Bush issued a Military Order authorizing the Department of Defense to create military commissions to try non-citizens who are members of [the Afghanistan military organization] al Qaeda or who have attempted or carried out acts of international terrorism. The promulgation of the order was met with overwhelming public support, but with a stream of criticism from civil libertarians and others concerned with the possible dilution of due process standards. The Military Order has also sparked a lively debate among lawyers and pundits in the op-ed columns of America's newspapers focusing on the legality of the commissions under international law and their actual utility in fighting terrorism.

What has unfortunately been missing from this debate is its proper political context. The question is not whether a military commission is a good or bad thing, but whether any adequate mechanism currently exists for prosecuting prisoners who end up in U.S. custody during the new terror war facing America and its allies. The narrow legalistic debate has failed so far to do justice to the magnitude and nature of the threat of terror war and the policy context for the decision to use military commissions. In this broader context, it becomes clear that current domestic and international mechanisms cannot respond effectively to the needs encountered in the current terror war, but that military commissions, properly used, can do so at least for now. In the longer run, the existing Yugoslav tribunal offers substantial promise as an international terrorism court for particular types of cases. But in the meantime, the need for an effective mechanism is acute, and the military commissions provide one.

A major policy shift

The current debate over military commissions is so intense and widespread that it gives inordinate importance to the question of the forum in which terrorists should be tried. In reality, courts, in whatever form, have only a small role in the terror war currently underway. The campaign of terror war directed against the United States can be described as "unconventional warfare conducted by unprivileged combatants with the assistance of criminal co-conspirators designed primarily to terrorize and kill civilians."

This campaign has been underway for nearly a decade and will likely continue well into the foreseeable future. The potential use of military tribunals was not intended and should not be seen as an effort to shortcut court procedures ordinarily applicable to individuals charged with crimes. Rather, it was intended as a major shift in policy away from the criminal law model as a means for deterring and preventing terrorism. Until September 11, 2001, when al Qaeda struck American targets, including the World Trade Center (in 1993), President Bill Clinton promised to hunt down those responsible and "bring them to justice." Unfortunately, he meant this literally: He called in the FBI as lead agency, and turned to federal prosecutors as the means for fulfilling his pledge. Naturally, no issue of where to prosecute terrorists arose, because in those few instances when the U.S. was able to arrest a terrorist, criminal trials were the principal means intended to "bring them to justice."

The domestic system has proven unable to deter and rarely able even to punish those responsible for terror crimes.

President Bush put all that behind him after the attacks of September 11. He called the attacks "acts of war," and demanded that the Taliban surrender [terrorist] Osama bin Laden and other al Qaeda leaders on pain of being treated the same as they, as "enemies" of the United States. When the Taliban refused, hailing bin Laden as a Muslim "hero," Bush (with Congress's support) attacked Afghanistan with military force and turned to the Department of Defense to lead the campaign. The terror war, long pursued by al Qaeda, was finally confronted as an issue of national security, rather than one of criminal law enforcement.

Taking his cue from this major shift in policy, Attorney General John Ashcroft, along with FBI Director Robert S. Mueller III, issued instructions to their personnel to implement a corresponding shift in focus, away from the investigation of terrorism as crimes and the preparation of criminal cases to the overriding objective of preventing terrorist attacks. (CIA Director George Tenet issued an analogous instruction.) Many of the anti-terrorist measures taken by the attorney general since then—some deservedly controversial—are part of this shift in policy designed to prevent terrorist acts through various forms of preemptive action.

It should be no surprise that, among the measures adopted that reflect the shift of policy from criminal law enforcement to military engagement, was the order instructing the Department of Defense, now the lead agency in the nation's effort, to set up military commissions to try terrorist fighters. Viewed as a national security problem, the al Qaeda network and the Taliban fighters constituted a force of some 40,000 to 50,000 men. A successful military engagement was certain to result in the capture and potential trial of hundreds, perhaps thousands, of individuals. The military commission was a mechanism far more suitable to meet this need than the full-blown trials used to prosecute conventional crimes in the federal courts.

The U.S. military rapidly responded to the new policy by engaging in a comprehensive use of force intended to bring about a victory and to end America's vulnerability to al Qaeda. To accomplish this objective, the military developed new doctrines, deployed advanced technological resources, embraced the extensive use of special forces, and selectively relied on assistance offered by our allies without compromising American leadership in the campaign. The intelligence community is also undertaking a critical reassessment of its capabilities and intelligence assets and is retooling to better meet the threat posed by al Qaeda.

The advantages of military commissions

Unlike the executive branch departments, the judicial system cannot rapidly retool or evolve to accommodate the new needs of terror war. The American domestic criminal system was designed primarily to protect civil liberties while effectively prosecuting those responsible for murder and other domestic crimes. The system was never intended or designed to perform the judicial roles related to terror war or for that matter to prevent fundamentalist terrorism. The creation of military commissions is thus an effort by the Bush administration to provide a method for trying non-citizen terrorists that corresponds to the shift from fighting terrorism with conventional law enforcement to serious foreign military engagement.

Just as a single cruise missile attack against near-empty training camps constituted ineffective, pinprick engagement, the use of the domestic criminal system to try all terrorist prisoners would amount to ineffective, pinprick justice. The domestic criminal justice system, by itself, is simply unable to serve as an effective tool in dealing with the judicial fallout of terror war. Even the most successful prosecutor of terrorists, U.S. Attorney Mary Jo White, has recognized that, with proper safeguards, military commissions "could be preferable to conventional trials in a time of war," as she told the *New York Times*.

The reasons for the preference for military commissions are numerous. First, and most important, the acts of terror committed by al Qaeda against civilians are not the types of crimes our domestic system was designed to prosecute; rather, as President Bush characterized them, they are war crimes. Senator Joseph Lieberman, writing in the *Washington Post* January 1, 2002, put it this way: "The attacks of September 11 were acts of war. Because they were carried out against defenseless civilians by terrorists posing as noncombatants using concealed weapons, the perpetrators were guilty of heinous war crimes, not simple domestic crimes."

Second, the domestic system has proven unable to deter and rarely able even to punish those responsible for terror crimes. In the cases of the Yemen hotel bombing, the attack on the Saudi National Guard, the 1996 Khobar Towers attack, the 1993 bombing of the World Trade Center, the 1998 bombings of U.S. embassies in Africa, and the U.S.S. Cole attack in 2000, the U.S. either has been unable to prosecute any responsible party or has prosecuted only a handful of low-level culprits and ideological supporters.

A military commission or some other judicial mechanism is the most appropriate means for determining their guilt or innocence.

Third, to insist on the application of American constitutional due process standards to terrorist perpetrators of war crimes would limit the U.S. in exercising its national security powers. Evidence subject to exclusion from a trial would not be appropriate to consider, even though the evidence was reliable and established heinous and ongoing behavior. Guilt would have to be established on the basis of such admissible evidence, beyond a reasonable doubt. The need to establish such proof, we are told, led to a catastrophic decision by the Clinton administration. In 1996, Sudan offered to detain and transfer bin Laden to the United States. According to the *Washington Post*, then-National Security Advisor Sandy Berger declined the offer on the grounds that it would not be possible to try and convict him in an American criminal court. This, despite our having no moral doubt of his involvement in the Yemen hotel bombing, the attack on the National Guard, and the Khobar Towers attack, and despite our awareness of his determination to engage in future attacks.

Fourth, extensive use of domestic courts may significantly undermine the United States' ability to protect its citizens and to prevent additional attacks. Judges and juries in such cases have historically been at risk from terrorist groups. Under current law, it is not possible to protect intelligence methods and information used against the defendants in court. While federal legislation limits the ability of defense counsel to examine intelligence agency files used to prepare a case, all information used in court, and all methods used to gather it, are open to the public. Even much of the unclassified information presented at trial may be of use to future terrorists—such as structural diagrams of the World Trade Center and expert testimony as to the size of an airplane necessary to bring down one of the towers.

The limitations of domestic courts in punishing and deterring those responsible for war crimes has apparently led United States officials to attempt to evade their own judicial system. For example, when Berger turned down Sudan's offer for bin Laden, he tried to persuade Saudi Arabia to take him and after a streamlined trial to have him hanged. According to a *New York Times* report, the Clinton administration sought to circumvent the rules of the American judicial system by persuading "friendly intelligence services to arrange the arrest and transfer of al Qaeda members without formal extradition or legal proceedings" to Egypt and other countries to stand trial.

Military commissions are fair and flexible

For the cases where an American citizen or an individual under protection of the U.S. Constitution is suspected of participation in war crimes against the United States, Congress has the authority to create a special District Court that can be designed so as to protect the defendant's constitutional rights while mitigating some of the concerns expressed above. For suspected war criminals and terrorists not under the protection of the U.S. Constitution—which to date is every individual detained by the United States in Afghanistan save one—a military commission or some other judicial mechanism is the most appropriate means for determining their guilt or innocence.

The military commission is able to avoid the shortcomings of the conventional judicial system because it is specifically designed to respond to situations in which the United States finds itself, during or as a result of a military engagement, in physical custody of non-U.S. citizens believed to be members of terrorist networks who have committed terror acts against the United States. The military commission would also be useful in dealing with individuals associated with institutions or governments, such as leading members of the former Taliban government, who aided and abetted those committing or planning terrorist acts against the United States and its allies.

Military commissions are a flexible tool on which the United States can rely to ascertain with relative informality which defendants are in fact responsible for criminal acts and which are not. This flexibility is an important, practical necessity; for example, in addition to the nearly 500 suspects in American custody by January 2002, Afghan forces were holding nearly 3,000 non-Afghan prisoners who may have had some connection to al Qaeda or may have been trained in terrorism. The military commissions also offer an opportunity—not possible in the domestic context—to create mixed tribunals involving civilian or military judges from countries such as Afghanistan and Pakistan, which currently exercise custody over the detainees, or from countries such as Saudi Arabia and Kuwait, whose citizens are among the detainees.

Contrary to some contentions, the military commissions can provide a full and fair trial while also protecting sensitive intelligence and other information crucial to further efforts to prevent and deter acts of terrorism and war crimes. The Department of Defense must (and we believe it will) ensure that the military commissions comply with the obligation in the Military Order to provide for a full and fair trial, and to ensure that the purpose of the commissions remains to ascertain the guilt or innocence of those accused of war crimes and terrorism. Given that all of the suspects to be tried by military commission will be foreign nationals, it is appropriate for the United States to look to international standards of justice in formulating procedures. Various sets of international standards exist, but the most practical are those used by the International Criminal Tribunal for Yugoslavia (ICTY). According to the statute and rules of evidence and procedure for the tribunal—formulated with the participation and approval of many nations and the entire U.N. Security Council—all defendants are entitled to an expeditious, fair, and public trial, the presumption of innocence, the right to defense counsel of their choosing or to have legal assistance provided, the right to examine evidence and witnesses, and the right not to be compelled to testify against oneself or to confess guilt.

International standards of justice, however, are not identical to those found in the U.S. Constitution or in the Federal Rules of Criminal Procedure. In fact, a number of constitutional protections applicable in U.S. criminal cases have been considered unnecessary or undesirable by the international community or have been significantly modified when applied in the international context for the purposes of ascertaining the guilt or innocence of those charged with war crimes. International standards do not bar hearsay, but rather permit the introduction of any relevant evidence which the court deems to have probative value, and there are no Fourth Amendment-style search and seizure restrictions. Trial by jury is not required. Under certain circumstances, witnesses against the accused may testify anonymously (using voice and image-altering technology) or submit their testimony in writing—thus significantly limiting the defendant's ability to cross-examine witnesses effectively. The prosecution may appeal acquittals (during which time the defendants usually remain in custody) and may seek to retry acquitted defendants if new information becomes available which pertains to guilt—thus exposing such defendants to double jeopardy by U.S. standards. A defendant may even be subject to a form of mini-trial in absentia when the prosecutor, unable to secure his presence, presents the evidence against the defendant in a public hearing for the purpose of reconfirming the indictment.

> *Courts, in whatever form, play only a small role in the fight against terror.*

International standards also provide for the strict protection of confidential and classified information as well as intelligence sources and methods. For instance, if the ICTY prosecutor is in possession of information obtained on a confidential basis, and which has been used solely for the purpose of generating new evidence, that initial information and its origin need not be disclosed by the prosecutor. If the government providing the information consents, the information may be used in the court—in a closed proceeding—but there is no requirement that the sources or methods be available for examination, or even disclosed to the defendant. The defendant is also not entitled to access to information in the possession of the prosecutor, the disclosure of which may prejudice further investigations, may be contrary to the public interest, or may affect the security interests of any state. These protections go beyond those provided in U.S. domestic law, which limit the scope of material defendants may request from intelligence agencies but do not protect sources and methods. In addition, as all court proceedings are open to the public, any information used in court automatically becomes available in the public domain.

At the Yugoslavia and Rwanda tribunals, a determination of guilt is made by a majority of the Trial Chamber, with the standard of proof being beyond a reasonable doubt. While these international courts may not impose the death penalty, over 130 states do—in particular for war crimes and terrorism—and the death penalty was imposed in a number of instances by the Nuremberg and Tokyo tribunals.

The draft rules under consideration by the Department of Defense are consistent with these international standards. The rules are reported to provide for appellate review, the presumption of innocence, the requirement of proof beyond a reasonable doubt to establish guilt, the admission of hearsay evidence (but with the application of the reasonable-person standard), the limited use of in camera proceedings, and the requirement of a unanimous decision for a sentence of death. . . .

Building on the Yugoslavia tribunal

A more pragmatic approach to creating an international mechanism that could supplement the use of military tribunals, and one that could have the advantage of displacing the International Criminal Court (ICC), would be to add to the jurisdiction of the existing ICTY crimes associated with terror wars no matter where or by whom they are committed. This could be accomplished through a U.N. Security Council resolution citing the authority of Chapter VII of the U.N. Charter, "Action with Respect to Threats to the Peace, Breaches of the Peace, and Acts of Aggression." The Security Council would have to markedly increase the ICTY's budget to provide for the hiring of a substantial number of personnel, in addition to modifying its organizational structure and mandating a number of overdue institutional reforms.

Transforming the ICTY to deal with certain terrorist crimes is preferable to creating a new international mechanism for a number of reasons. After nearly eight years of operation the ICTY has an established set of rules of procedure and evidence and has a rational jurisprudence. The tribunal is perceived as fair and capable, with a competent prosecutor and a solid complement of trial and appellate judges, including a number of Islamic judges. The tribunal was in fact originally created in response to atrocities and war crimes committed against Muslims because of their religious identity. The tribunal should thus have a heightened degree of credibility among those who might otherwise be skeptical of an international tribunal. Moreover, as an institution with ample independence, yet created and supported by the Security Council and subject to its continuing review, the transformed Yugoslavia tribunal would avoid many of the political and practical afflictions of the ICC. While a U.S. military commission could be used to try most suspected terrorists and war criminals, the expanded Yugo/terrorism tribunal could be used to try top-level suspects and those who do not come into U.S. custody.

Bearing in mind that courts, in whatever form, play only a small role in the fight against terror, the recent authorization of the use of military commissions should be welcomed as a sign that the U.S. government will not continue the criminal-law response to terror war, which contributed to the vulnerability of the United States on September 11. Assuming that the rules of procedure and evidence for the commissions comply with international standards, the commissions will fill a crucial role, one that the domestic criminal justice system is incapable of meeting. In addition, the United States should initiate an effort in the Security Council to expand the existing Yugoslavia tribunal to enable it to prosecute certain particularly egregious terrorist crimes. This would have the dual benefit of creating a viable mechanism to aid in the war against terror, and supplanting the ICC, which is likely to restrict efforts of the United States and its current allies to protect themselves and their interests against future acts of terrorism amounting to acts of war. In this way, courts and the rule of law will serve to make the battle for freedom more rather than less effective.

8

Military Commissions Are Unwise and Unconstitutional

Diane F. Orentlicher and Robert Kogod Goldman

Diane F. Orentlicher and Robert Kogod Goldman are law professors at American University in Washington, D.C.

Military commissions are the wrong method for prosecuting suspected terrorists. Acts of terrorism that occur during peacetime cannot be considered war crimes and therefore cannot be tried under military law. Because the defendants are considered enemies by the U.S. military, it is unlikely that these commissions—composed of military personnel—will be impartial and objective. The commissions also do not guarantee defendants important rights, such as the right to counsel and the right to avoid self-incrimination. Federal courts are a more appropriate venue for prosecuting terrorists.

The terrorist attacks of September 11, 2001, triggered an intense debate that continues to the present day: were they monstrous crimes—or acts of war? Should the U.S. response be shaped by a military or criminal justice paradigm? Framed this way, the debate poses a classic false dichotomy. The international community has strongly supported the United States in its claim that the September 11 attacks constituted an armed attack justifying military action against the Al Qaeda network and its Taliban sponsors in Afghanistan. At the same time, other countries are working hand in hand with U.S. law enforcement agencies in a criminal investigation of global sweep.

But if crimes of terrorism can also be acts of war, it is a mistake to conflate the two. President George W. Bush's November 13, 2001 Military Order authorizing military commissions to prosecute suspected terrorists does just that, treating virtually any foreign national whom the President suspects of terrorist-related activity as an enemy belligerent, regardless of whether the United States is engaged in armed conflict. In doing so, the Military Order exceeds the President's constitutional authority to estab-

Excerpted from "When Justice Goes to War: Prosecuting Terrorists Before Military Commissions," by Diane F. Orentlicher and Robert Kogod Goldman, *Harvard Journal of Law*, Spring 2002. Copyright © 2002 by Harvard Society for Law and Public Policy, Inc. Reprinted with permission.

lish military commissions and imperils core constitutional values.

Even when legally permissible, military commissions are generally an unwise choice among the options available for trying those believed to be responsible for the attacks of September 11 and other crimes of terrorism. Far better to try them before federal courts, as the United States has successfully done as recently as [2002] in connection with two other horrific crimes committed by members of Al Qaeda—the 1998 terrorist attacks on U.S. embassies in Kenya and Tanzania.

The legality of military commissions

A fundamental feature of the Military Order is that it invokes presidential war powers to support the prosecution of suspected terrorists before military commissions. Citing the President's constitutional authority as Commander in Chief of the armed forces, the Order provides that the President may order certain individuals to be detained by the Secretary of Defense and to be prosecuted exclusively before military commissions "for violations of the laws of war and other applicable laws by military tribunals."

But in a legal and conceptual non-sequitur, the Order defines its field of application in terms of individuals whom the President suspects of participation in international terrorism, a term the Order nowhere defines, against the United States. Thus the President seeks to detain suspected terrorists on the basis of his authority to prosecute war criminals. Like the figures in M.C. Escher's lithograph "Verbum" that morph from frogs into birds and then fishes, the President's order shifts from one legal paradigm to another.

For reasons we explain in the next section, this aspect of the Military Order renders much of the Order constitutionally flawed. More particularly, the Military Order exceeds the province of presidential war powers when it purports to subject civilians in the United States to trial before military commissions because they may have supported Al Qaeda operatives or other individuals suspected of participation in international terrorism. When acts of terrorism take place in peacetime, as they frequently do, they are not triable as war crimes under international law and the President cannot make them so by the stroke of a pen.

Even when legally permissible, military commissions are generally an unwise choice.

The principal federal law cited in support of the Military Order contemplates the possibility of convening military commissions "with respect to offenders or offenses that by statute or by the law of war may be tried by military commission." In U.S. law and practice, military commissions, courts, and tribunals have four distinct types of jurisdiction, of which only two are relevant here—"martial law" and "law of war" jurisdiction.

Although the scope of martial law jurisdiction is contested, it generally applies when the President directs the military to exercise judicial authority in parts of the country where the civilian court system is no longer functioning due to war, insurrection, or a comparable disaster. The

Military Order is carefully scored with this theme, asserting, for example, that future terrorist attacks "may place at risk the continuity of the operations of the United States government."

But the leading case on martial law jurisdiction, Ex parte Milligan, makes clear that this risk would not justify the exercise of military jurisdiction over U.S. citizens, and indeed the Military Order explicitly applies only to non-citizens. In Milligan, the Supreme Court held unconstitutional the trial of a citizen of Indiana by a military commission convened in Indianapolis during the Civil War. In the words of the Court majority, military jurisdiction that is founded on the "laws and usages of war . . . can never be applied to citizens in states which have upheld the authority of the government, and where the courts are open and their process unobstructed," unless the citizens are members of the armed forces.

The Court recognized that there are circumstances in which martial rule can be imposed, but the contemporary threat of terrorism does not meet the Court's stringent test:

> If, in foreign invasion or civil war, the courts are actually closed, and it is impossible to administer criminal justice according to law, then, on the theatre of active military operations, where war really prevails, there is a necessity to furnish a substitute for the civil authority, thus overthrown, to preserve the safety of the army and society; and as no power is left but the military, it is allowed to govern by martial rule until the laws can have their free course.

But, the Court continued, "martial rule can never exist where the courts are open, and in the proper and unobstructed exercise of their jurisdiction. It is also confined to the locality of actual war."

Trial by jury

It is not hard to see why the right to trial by jury was jealously guarded by the Supreme Court, even in respect to a defendant charged with conspiring to overthrow federal authority by force of arms when the nation was at war. Against the claim that recourse to martial law was justified by the imperatives of security in war time, the Court replied: "Civil liberty and this kind of martial law cannot endure together; the antagonism is irreconcilable; and, in the conflict, one or the other must perish."

At the proverbial first blush, President Bush's order finds stronger support in Ex parte Quirin, a leading U.S. case on "laws of war" jurisdiction of military commissions. This 1942 Supreme Court decision arose out of the surreptitious entry into the United States of eight German saboteurs (one of whom may have possessed U.S. citizenship) bearing explosives and incendiary devices. Acting under instruction from the German High Command, the eight apparently intended to destroy war industries and facilities in the United States. Soon after their arrival and capture, President Franklin D. Roosevelt issued an order authorizing the trial of the saboteurs before a military tribunal.

Upholding the lawfulness of the saboteurs' trial, the Supreme Court distinguished Milligan on the ground that the defendants "were charged with an offense against the law of war which the Constitution does not require to be tried by jury." Crucial to this conclusion was the Court's finding that the petitioners were "unlawful combatants" since they operated as enemy combatants "without uniform or other appropriate means of identification."

Under international law, the Court reasoned, unlawful combatants "are subject to trial and punishment by military tribunals for acts which render their belligerency unlawful." In the Court's view, constitutional guarantees of trial by jury and presentment to a grand jury were not intended to enlarge the scope of these rights as they existed at common law, and unlawful belligerents had long been subject to military jurisdiction.

Much like the Supreme Court's validation of President Roosevelt's decision to intern American citizens of Japanese descent during World War II, Quirin has long been criticized as an abdication of independent judicial judgment during war time and an unwarranted surrender of constitutional rights. Even the author of the Court's opinion, Chief Justice Stone, reportedly had grave misgivings about the judgment he penned.

The Military Order is utterly inconsistent with the international legal obligations of the United States.

But even if the authority of Quirin were beyond question, it would provide only limited support for President Bush's Order. At most, Quirin supports the use of military commissions to try those responsible for the September 11 attacks and others suspected of violating the laws of war that, by definition, can occur only in the course of armed conflict. Like the German saboteurs of 1942, the men who hijacked four civilian aircraft and transformed them into human missiles can fairly be regarded as unprivileged combatants. In the context of the armed conflict in Afghanistan, the United States could treat Al Qaeda as a paramilitary organization and its members as unprivileged combatants who do not observe the basic rules of warfare as required by Article 4A(2) of the Third Geneva Convention of 1949. As unprivileged combatants, Quirin holds, these individuals are not entitled to the constitutional protections of presentment to a grand jury and trial by jury.

But President Bush's Military Order reaches far beyond the authority sustained in Quirin, authorizing the detention and trial before military commissions of any alien whom the President determines at his sole discretion has "aided or abetted" terrorism that has injured or potentially could injure U.S. citizens or a broad class of U.S. interests or who the President believes may have "harbored" a terrorist. Moreover the Order imposes no temporal limit on conduct that can be lawfully scrutinized and judged by these tribunals.

Thus, for example, a long-term resident alien who in 1998 gave money, directly or indirectly, to Al Qaeda but had no involvement in the September 11 attacks could be deemed an aider and abetter and thus detained on the authority of the Military Order. But these individuals cannot be tried for violations of the laws of war when no state of hostilities, de facto or de jure, existed as between the U.S. and Al Qaeda before September 11.

It remains to be noted that the Military Order, which finds its principal support in the precedent of Quirin, defies Quirin itself by purporting to deny persons detained pursuant to the Order the right "to seek any remedy or maintain any proceeding, directly or indirectly, or to have any such remedy or proceeding sought on the individual's behalf, in . . . any court of the United States." This provision substantially tracks language in the presidential proclamation underlying the trial of German saboteurs during World War II. Yet the Supreme Court had no trouble concluding that the saboteurs could have recourse to federal court to challenge the lawfulness of their prosecution before a military commission.

Insufficient safeguards

Our discussion in the previous section focused on whether the Military Order exceeds the President's authority to convene military commissions. An equally important question is whether individuals prosecuted under the authority of the Order will be afforded procedural safeguards required by international law.

Insofar as it permits civilians to be tried by such commissions, the Military Order is utterly inconsistent with the international legal obligations of the United States. Human rights instruments binding on the United States mandate that criminal defendants, whatever their offenses, be tried by independent and impartial courts that afford generally recognized due process guarantees. By their very nature, military commissions do not satisfy this basic test. The military justice system in the U.S. and elsewhere is not part of the independent civilian judiciary, but rather is part of the Executive Branch. Under the Military Order, the U.S. military, which is also charged with the destruction of terrorists on the battlefield, would become the prosecutor and judge of its alleged adversaries.

U.S. courts are fully capable of meeting the challenges presented by cases involving terrorism.

When active duty military officers assume the role of judges, they remain subordinate to their superiors in keeping with the established military hierarchy. The manner by which they fulfill their assigned task might well play a role in their future promotions, assignments, and professional rewards. It is because of this inherent dependence that these tribunals are not suited to try civilians. And where, as here, the putative defendants before these military commissions are the military's avowed enemies, these tribunals cannot reasonably be expected to be, nor will they be seen as, objective finders of fact and dispensers of impartial justice. Similar considerations have led the Inter-American Commission and Court of Human Rights, as well as the U.N. Human Rights Committee, to find that the use of military courts to try civilians in Guatemala, Peru, Chile, Uruguay and elsewhere violated fundamental due process rights. Moreover, no human rights supervisory body has yet found the exigencies of a genuine emergency situation, such as that now faced by the U.S., to justify suspending basic fair trial safeguards even on a temporary basis.

The rights that must be accorded to unprivileged combatants in criminal proceedings have evolved substantially since World War II. Any doubts concerning the scope and content of these rights were put to rest with the elaboration of Article 75 of Protocol I Additional to the 1949 Geneva Conventions. Although the United States has not ratified the Protocol, it accepts many of its provisions as being declaratory of customary law; Article 75 is such a provision par excellence. Largely inspired by human rights law, this article requires that unprivileged combatants be accorded in all circumstances trials by impartial and regularly constituted courts that, at a minimum, afford inter alia ["among other things"] the presumption of innocence, the right to counsel before and during trial, the right of defendants to call witnesses and to examine witnesses against them, freedom from ex post facto laws, and the right of defendants not to testify against themselves or to confess their guilt.

President Bush's Military Order does not even purport to provide these safeguards. Although the Order states that defendants before military commissions shall be granted a full and fair trial, it does not expressly guarantee the presumption of innocence or the right of defendants to counsel of their choice; it denies defendants any remedy, including appeal and habeas corpus, to either a U.S. or international court; and it potentially bars defendants from seeing the evidence against them. In light of these deficiencies, Spain has indicated that it may not extradite to the United States individuals it has charged with complicity in the September 11 attacks without assurances that they will be tried by civilian courts and not be subject to the death penalty. Other European Union (EU) member states, which are parties to European human rights treaties, are expected to follow suit.

The problematic features of the Military Order could be addressed through procedural rules governing the conduct of trials before military commissions. Yet draft regulations described in media accounts in late December 2001 go only part of the way toward addressing these concerns.

Federal courts are a better solution

The thrust of international fair trial standards . . . is to ensure that all persons charged with criminal offenses, including unprivileged combatants, not be tried in a rush to judgment in the kind of summary proceedings contemplated in the Military Order. Thus even where military commissions might be lawfully available, such as in respect to unprivileged combatants, defendants must be afforded the safeguards recognized in Article 75 of Additional Protocol I. If the Bush administration insists on using military commissions to try some unprivileged combatants, the Military Order should be amended to allow civilian review of convictions and sentences. This would provide a crucial check against the inherent risk of partiality of military judges who are charged with evaluating the guilt of their avowed enemies.

But another approach, trial before federal courts, is far preferable. Recent convictions of members of the Al Qaeda network show that U.S. courts are fully capable of meeting the challenges presented by cases involving terrorism, including those relating to the use of classified evidence. Some commentators have argued, however, that trying terrorists in federal court may unfairly expose jurors to intimidation. To the extent this is a valid concern, Quirin points the way to a solution. Since, according to Quirin, unprivileged combatants are not constitutionally entitled to trial by jury, they could be tried before a federal judge if the risk of juror intimidation were substantial. Above all, the deepest interests of this nation counsel us to stay the hand of military justice: to renounce federal court jurisdiction over crimes of terror is to concede a powerful victory to those bent on destroying cherished symbols of our national life.

9

A Missile Defense System Would Ensure National and Global Security

Richard Perle

Richard Perle is a resident fellow at the American Enterprise Institute, an organization that advocates national defense and a strong foreign policy, and a former assistant secretary for international security policy at the Defense Department.

One of the best ways for the United States to protect lives here and throughout the world is to build a missile defense system that would be capable of intercepting ballistic missiles sent by enemy nations. This approach to defense is a significant improvement over the 1972 Anti-Ballistic Missile (ABM) Treaty and the Cold War attitudes of President Bill Clinton's administration, both of which have resulted in the United States being unable to defend itself in the event of a devastating nuclear attack. Despite the claims of some European critics, the ABM Treaty no longer serves American or Western interests and should be overturned.

The question is not *whether* a ballistic missile with a nuclear or chemical or biological warhead capable of killing hundreds of thousands of Americans will wind up in the hands of a hostile power. The question is *when*.

Pinpointing the exact date is a game played by intelligence agencies, rather like an office pool on the outcome of the Super Bowl. In the Super Bowl, though, you at least know who the players are. When it comes to the acquisition of a ballistic missile or a nuclear warhead, there is no sure way of telling.

That is why it is so urgent we begin now to build a system capable of intercepting the missile that we know is coming. The argument for getting on with it is overwhelming. The arguments against are unconvincing—and drawn mostly from ideas that developed during the Cold War but have been rendered irrelevant by its end.

From "New Weapon for a New World Order," by Richard Perle, *American Enterprise*, April/May 2001. Copyright © 2001 by the American Enterprise, a magazine of Politics, Business, and Culture. Reprinted with permission.

Missile defense systems save lives

The best argument in favor of building a missile defense system is a moral one: It will save lives, in large numbers, in other countries as well as our own. It will discourage the proliferation of missiles and warheads of mass destruction. It will make the world stabler and safer.

Consider the following scenario, for example. Imagine a sharp rise in tension between traditional adversaries India and Pakistan, both of which have nuclear weapons and ballistic missiles. Suppose the United States Navy could dispatch an Aegis cruiser to the region with instructions to intercept any ballistic missile fired by either side. Such a capability in American hands would be highly stabilizing, discouraging hair-trigger missile attacks, reducing the likelihood of conflict breaking out in the first place, reassuring both sides.

Nations like Iran, Iraq, and North Korea are trying to acquire long-range missiles. They believe that possessing even a single missile will catapult them into a select class of powers, gaining great leverage because they will be capable of inflicting massive damage on the United States or its friends and allies. And given time and money, these countries *can* reasonably hope to possess a single missile, or even several.

But suppose we constructed a defense that could intercept all the warheads and decoys carried by 100 or 200 enemy missiles. A Saddam Hussein in Iraq or a Kim Jong Il in North Korea would lose any confidence he could land a missile on New York or Chicago or an allied capital. The relatively easy task of acquiring a missile or two would become the impossible burden of acquiring hundreds.

In that case, even a determined adversary is likely to throw up his hands and conclude that enhancing his power with nuclear long-range missiles is simply too hard. Imagine a meeting of Saddam Hussein with his military advisors. The general in charge of Iraq's armored force pleads for money to buy new tanks and spare parts for old ones, while the general in charge of missile development requests billions of dollars for construction and testing of a new missile. If the United States has the ability to defend itself and its allies against 100 such missiles, how does the general in charge of the missile program answer Saddam's question, "What good is a $10 billion missile if the Americans can knock it down?"

In short, the best way to protect against missile dangers is to discourage our adversaries from investing in the missiles in the first place. There can be no more powerful disincentive than to have a shield that guarantees their hugely expensive programs will fail. It is that shield, based on our most advanced technology, that will protect America best—not the flotsam of the 1972 Anti-Ballistic Missile (ABM) Treaty to which the opponents of missile defense cling like shipwrecked sailors.

The history of an obsolete treaty

Some Americans still treat the ABM Treaty with reverence. It remains a primary obstacle to our going forward with missile defense, so a short history lesson is needed to explain why the treaty is hopelessly obsolete.

Cold War nuclear theology held that if one side were to deploy a defense against ballistic missiles, the other side would simply build more missiles in numbers sufficient to overwhelm the defense. Thus the specter of an arms race, often described as an "ever upward spiral," became a central theme in foreign offices and ministries of defense around the world.

So, in 1972 the United States and the Soviet Union signed a treaty banning the deployment of national missile defenses. Reflecting the logic of the Cold War, the ABM Treaty sought to assure each side that the other was vulnerable to a retaliatory missile attack. Given the deep political, ideological, and military divisions between the superpowers at that time, the notion gained currency that vulnerability to a missile attack with many nuclear weapons was a good thing. This "Mutual Assured Destruction" would keep anyone from attacking and thus make us safe.

[A missile defense system] will save lives, in large numbers, in other countries as well as our own.

Though it prohibits the deployment of a national missile defense, the ABM Treaty does allow certain research short of deployment, as well as the actual deployment of no more than 100 interceptor missiles at a single location in each country. The Russians long ago built such a system around Moscow, which they maintain today. The United States, which abandoned its own fledgling system after the 1972 treaty, has none.

In April 1983, President Ronald Reagan announced a new program of research and development to determine whether the United States could build an effective defense against ballistic missiles. The initiative was vehemently opposed by the Soviet Union, by many American intellectuals, and by anxious Europeans. Following the 1983 announcement, a succession of Soviet leaders tried to negotiate further restrictions on the deployment of defensive systems. The most important such negotiation took place in Iceland in 1986 at a summit meeting between President Reagan and Communist Party Secretary Mikhail Gorbachev. The Reykjavik summit ended when President Reagan refused to accept Soviet proposals to confine further development of missile defenses to the laboratory, a technological straitjacket which would have throttled any serious defense in its infancy.

A Cold War mind-set

Because we cling to an obsolete treaty with a nation that no longer exists, the United States stands naked today before its enemies, unable to intercept even a single ballistic missile aimed, by accident or design, at our territory. Many Americans are shocked to learn that this condition of abject vulnerability is the freely chosen policy of the government of the United States and widely insisted upon by America's allies.

Frozen in the Cold War like a fly in amber, the Clinton administration's policies were based on the outdated idea that our exposure to attack by ballistic missiles actually made us safer. Clintonites argued the vulnerability that developed during the Cold War should become a permanent feature of American policy, enshrined in a trivially modified—and thereby reinvigorated—ABM Treaty.

Under political pressure in 2000 not to cede the issue of missile defense to the Republicans, President Bill Clinton toyed with deployment of a manifestly inadequate system in Alaska that could not protect all of the U.S. or *any* of our allies. It was a system designed more to remain within the confines of the ABM Treaty than to actually defend the country. Clinton chose to develop a system so modest and ineffective as to be useless for all but political purposes.

Mired in Cold War thinking, the Clinton administration argued that a technologically serious defense, even if limited, would precipitate an arms race. The administration actually assured the Russians in meetings that even if the U.S. built an effective defense in Alaska, Russia would still be able to incinerate the United States at any time. It is hard to imagine a mind-set more reflective of the Cold War than that.

American and Western interests

The idea that the ABM Treaty is a cornerstone of stability is especially popular among America's European allies. But it seems fair to ask: How can a treaty that was the cornerstone of stability in 1972 remain our foundation [today]? After all, there is almost nothing in common between the geopolitical situation in the middle of the Cold War and the situation today. Former Secretary of State Henry Kissinger, who negotiated the ABM Treaty, has argued convincingly that it no longer serves American interests. I think that argument can be broadened to include Western interests generally.

Some Europeans have claimed that Europe could become a target of convenience if an American missile defense left potential adversaries unable to attack the U.S. directly. In this scenario, a Saddam Hussein or a Kim Jong Il might think, "If I can't destroy New York, I'll just have to destroy Berlin or Paris instead." I suppose one can't rule out such a development, though it surely is not high on the list of things French President Jacques Chirac or German Chancellor Gerhard Schroeder ought to be worrying about.

It is now terrorists and tyrants who threaten us, not empires, and we must therefore have more selective and sophisticated ways of defending ourselves.

The idea, though, gives rise to several thoughts. First, this bizarre concern shows that the Europeans recognize there may indeed be a threat from ballistic missiles in the hands of unpredictable, vindictive, malicious leaders. After hearing any number of learned Europeans tell us that there is no threat, or that we are overstating it, this is a welcome acknowledgment. Second, any missile defense we plan can and should cover our European allies. I believe the George W. Bush administration will think in those terms, even if the Clinton administration did not.

In any case, what are the Europeans expecting of us? Do they think their concerns will have America responding, "Oh, how silly of us to think we should defend ourselves. If you're worried that could put you in harm's way, we'll just drop the whole idea and remain vulnerable. We certainly would not want our defense to cause you any concern."

Consider: with no missile defense, even one incoming warhead could do catastrophic harm to Los Angeles or Washington or New York. A handful would mean destruction beyond imagination. Now, suppose we were to deploy a defense capable of countering not one or a handful, but a few hundred incoming warheads. With such a defense, we might no longer be vulnerable to such nuclear powers as, say, Great Britain or France, which have their own deterrent forces. Would the British then feel compelled to build more nuclear weapons to overpower our defense?

Of course not. Why not? *Because they don't regard the United States as an enemy.* They don't fear an American attack. (Actually the French do fear an attack but (a) it comes from Hollywood and not the U.S. military, (b) it is truly devastating, and (c) while Chirac may think our anti-missile system won't work, I *know* his defense against American culture will fail.) In other words, it is the political context, not the weapons themselves, that determines whether, and to what extent, any particular military capability is threatening.

Now that the Cold War is over, should Russia regard us as an enemy? We are more likely to send Mr. Putin a check than a barrage of missiles with nuclear warheads. We have sought in countless ways to work with, not against, the Russians. We have muted our criticism—wrongly in my view—of Russia's outrageous assault on civilians in Chechnya. It is unimaginable that we would launch thousands of nuclear weapons against Russia and hope to benefit thereby. And that would be true even if we had a defense that could knock down every missile that might be launched in retaliation.

Would it make sense for Mr. Putin to respond to an American defense against North Korea or Saddam Hussein by building more missiles? Is the Russian economy in a condition where such a vast investment in new weapons would benefit his country? And what about China? We recently sent them an invitation into the world trading system. Should they fear an American missile attack? Or regard an American defense as a threat to China? And even if they *did* think in these terms, should we remain vulnerable to all the world just to reassure *them*?

Sometimes we hear that perceptions, not reality, are what counts: If the Russians or the Chinese perceive the United States as a threat and therefore regard any anti-missile system we may build as a danger, shouldn't the U.S. stand down?

This seems a particularly unwise line of argument. In psychiatry it would lead to humoring paranoids by accepting their paranoia and acting to accommodate baseless fears. In science it would mean the abandonment of rigor and discipline, pretending instead of proving. And in international politics it would mean nurturing rather than finding ways to correct false, dangerous, and even self-fulfilling ideas.

The threat of terrorism

The final argument in favor of ballistic missile defense is an ethical one, and the most compelling: During the great clash of the Cold War, it may have been defensible to threaten to kill millions of innocents with nuclear weapons in order to deter massive Soviet attacks on the West. But it is not morally defensible now to say we will kill, say, tens of thousands of innocent men and women in Afghanistan if Osama bin Laden launches a single rather crude missile at Naples. It is now terrorists and tyrants who threaten us, not empires, and we must therefore have more selective and sophisticated ways of defending ourselves.

The Cold War is over, but we will not realize the full benefit of its passing until everyone involved behaves accordingly—abandoning the fears and apprehensions of half a century of conflict, and the outdated ideas about security that flowed from that long, dark struggle.

Clinging to the notion that the security of others is diminished if the United States is protected against missile attack only perpetuates the anxiety of the Cold War. And that is a climate we must transcend now—so that we may protect ourselves and our allies against the real threats we face today.

10

A Missile Defense System Would Not Protect National Security

David Cortright

David Cortright is the president of the Fourth Freedom Forum, a private foundation that addresses international security issues.

Missile defense is not the answer to reducing the threat of nuclear weapons. Instead, a national missile defense system, such as the one supported by President George W. Bush's administration, violates the 1972 Anti-Ballistic Missile Treaty and could undermine national and global security. If the United States deploys a national missile defense system, it will likely lead to the buildup of offensive nuclear weapons in Russia and China. In addition, missile defense does not protect against many terrorist threats. If the United States wishes to reduce the spread of nuclear weapons and ballistic missiles, particularly in North Korea, Iran, and Iraq, it should rely on diplomatic strategies instead of unproven technology.

A mong the curious twists of the debate on national missile defense is the trend among conservatives to condemn the immorality of nuclear weapons. In a "BreakPoint" commentary heard on 1,000 radio stations, Christian conservative Chuck Colson spoke of "the moral insanity" of mutual assured destruction. According to Colson, thoughtful people question the doctrine of nuclear deterrence because the threat to annihilate millions of innocent civilians is morally untenable.

It's gratifying that Colson and other conservatives have finally "got religion" on this point. But by coupling their condemnation of nuclear weapons with support for national missile defense, these conservatives undermine the integrity of their argument and put themselves back into the very same moral behind they seek to escape.

The global threat from weapons of mass destruction is indeed great, and it is increasing as nuclear weapons and ballistic missile capabilities spread to other countries. There are now eight nuclear weapons states—

the original five (United States, United Kingdom, Russia, France, and China), along with Israel (with an arsenal of more than 200 weapons) and the latest entries, India and Pakistan. Several other countries, including Iran and Iraq, have been or are currently engaged in nuclear weapons development. Finding a way to protect against these dangers is a moral imperative. But the answer does not lie in technology, especially one as unproven as missile defense.

The uselessness of missile defense systems

The pursuit of national missile defense could increase international tensions and spark a new arms race. Conservative analysts and George W. Bush administration officials argue that the 1972 Anti-Ballistic Missile (ABM) Treaty limiting missile defense systems is "ancient history" and should be scrapped. They want to rush ahead to deploy a national missile defense system, over the objections of Russia if necessary, in open violation of the ABM treaty. This would be an act of monumental folly that could seriously undermine U.S. and world security. Russia has repeatedly vowed to counter the deployment of a national missile defense with its own buildup of offensive nuclear weapons. Russia has also linked further progress on nuclear missile reduction to the continuation of the ABM treaty. China has also vowed to increase its offensive nuclear capabilities if the United States deploys a national missile defense.

The concept of a national missile defense system is premised on the possible threat of nuclear missile attack from "states of concern" such as North Korea or Iraq. But these dangers are grossly overstated, while the more likely threat of a low-level terrorist attack is unmet. A ballistic missile attack is one of the least likely threats facing the United States. If [Iraq president] Saddam Hussein or [terrorist] Osama bin Laden wanted to attack the United States, they would place their weapons in a truck or a ship container, not atop a ballistic missile. The proposed national missile defense system is useless against these threats.

The notion that North Korea, an impoverished nation unable to feed its citizens, could attack the United States with intercontinental ballistic missiles is far-fetched. North Korea is indeed a militarized state and has attempted to develop nuclear weapons and ballistic missiles, but its capabilities are extremely limited. It has attempted to launch multi-stage missiles only twice, and both tests were failures.

What has lessened the threat of a ballistic missile attack against the United States from what it was 15 or 20 years ago? The United States and Russia have reduced their nuclear missile arsenals by more than half since the end of the Cold War. Relations between Washington and Moscow have turned from hostility to cooperation across a broad range of activities—including the cooperative threat reduction program in which the United States is helping to dismantle the former Soviet nuclear arsenal. It is developments like these that make us more secure.

Relying on diplomacy

Why not apply the same approach of arms reduction and cooperative engagement to other nations that pose a potential threat? Instead of spending tens of billions of dollars in pursuit of an unproven technology in response to exaggerated threats, why not devote our energy and resources to improving political relations with other nations? The best guarantee of security is to turn enemies into friends. Diplomatic strategies offer a less costly means of reducing the threat of nuclear missile attack, with a higher assurance of genuine security.

The Korean peninsula may be one of the most promising examples of the effectiveness of diplomatic engagement as a means of reducing nuclear dangers. In 1994 North Korea and the United States negotiated the Agreed Framework that put an end to the North Korean nuclear production program. Under the terms of that agreement, North Korea agreed to halt its production of fissile materials, to end the reprocessing of spent nuclear fuel, and to open its nuclear facilities to on-site inspection. In return the United States and its partners (South Korea and Japan) agreed to supply the North with fuel oil and safer, less-proliferation-prone nuclear reactors and to begin the process of diplomatic engagement. The Agreed Framework has been a significant success. The North Korean nuclear production program was shut down and remains under international inspection today. The North Korean nuclear threat is effectively contained.

A ballistic missile attack is one of the least likely threats facing the United States.

A similar bargain is possible now with the North Korean ballistic missile program. North Korea has said repeatedly that it will give up the development of ballistic missiles in exchange for a lifting of U.S. economic sanctions and the normalization of diplomatic and commercial relations. The Bill Clinton administration partially lifted sanctions [in 2000] and came tantalizingly close to negotiating a missile agreement in its final days in office. Under the terms of the tentative agreement, North Korea would refrain from the testing of ballistic missiles and halt the transfer of such weapons to other countries. Such an arrangement would effectively end the missile threat from North Korea. President Bush has been urged to move quickly to close the deal, but he told visiting South Korean president Kim Dae Jung that his administration is in no hurry to resume negotiations with the North.

Diplomatic options for reducing the threat of weapons of mass destruction are also possible with Iran and Iraq. The United States has already taken tentative steps toward improving relations with the reform government in Iran. A lifting of U.S. economic sanctions could pave the way toward a genuine warming of political relations. In Iraq as well, a lifting of economic sanctions and the use of other incentives could help to resolve the impasse over the dismantling of Baghdad's weapons capabilities. No matter how seemingly intractable the dispute, strategies of diplomatic engagement have the potential to improve political relations and ease weapons-related tensions.

Of course, Washington could greatly enhance the effectiveness of U.S. diplomacy by fulfilling its obligations under the Non-Proliferation Treaty to eliminate its own nuclear weapons. Article VI of that treaty, as well as the preamble of the ABM treaty, commit the United States to the goal of nuclear weapons abolition. Despite this, the United States maintains more than 10,000 nuclear weapons, many of them deployed atop intercontinental ballistic missiles. It is unseemly and fundamentally unjust for the United States to insist that other countries give up their weapons while we cling to them as the bedrock of our defense. If we want to reduce the global missile threat, we must lead by example in lowering weapons stockpiles to zero and creating an alternative, non-nuclear security system.

Only a global ban on all nuclear weapons and their delivery systems can offer a morally consistent and politically effective means of protecting the innocent from the threat of weapons of mass destruction. The best protection is no nuclear weapons at all.

11

The Failures of Intelligence Agencies Have Threatened National Security

Andrew Roberts

Andrew Roberts is a historian and writer for several publications, including the Spectator, *the* Sunday Telegraph, *and* Literary Review.

Incompetence throughout American intelligence agencies was a major factor in the United States being unaware that terrorists were planning to attack the nation on September 11, 2001. In particular, the quality of intelligence gathering in the CIA has declined because the organization has few operatives who are able or willing to live in the Middle East among Muslim fundamentalists. Despite problems within the CIA and other intelligence agencies, such as the FBI and the National Security Agency, reform is unlikely, leaving the United States vulnerable to further terrorist attacks.

So where was Felix Leiter? In the James Bond movies the threatened climax is usually something as ghastly as the destruction of the World Trade Center, but that outcome is always averted by James and his competent and dependable CIA friend. Not this time. When Osama bin Laden's al-Qa'eda organisation was planning its spectacular attack on the heart of Western capitalism on September 11, 2001, Mr Leiter, it seems, was at his headquarters in Langley, Virginia, either on a sensitivity-training course or, perhaps, sewing a 'diversity quilt'. No fewer than 20,000 CIA man-hours have been spent on those activities in the past year.

Whatever Felix was doing, the CIA has now been forced to admit that it has been making systematic errors about security. Since 11 September academics, intelligence experts and former CIA and FBI officials—mainly but not exclusively of a conservative hue—have taken the Agency to task for putting political correctness and wishful thinking before operational efficiency. In stark contrast to the 'can do' ethos—the cloak-and-dagger derring-do—of the intelligence operations of the Fifties and Sixties, modern intelligence-gathering has been badly stymied by modish notions and 'due process'.

Key criticisms

Are the British intelligence agencies suffering from the same problems: is James Bond any better prepared than Felix was? It is true that the walls of MI6's Vauxhall headquarters are not hung with diversity quilts, but confidence in its power to protect us was severely dented when in 1999 our domestic intelligence agency MI5 failed to protect their colleagues on the South Bank from an Irish Republican Army (IRA) rocket attack launched across the Thames from a site virtually opposite the Tate Gallery. With my old Cambridge contemporary Richard Tomlinson posting the names of 115 MI6 operatives on the Web, and the former director-general of MI5, Stella Rimington, writing her memoirs, Britain's spooks do not inspire great confidence.

In assessing the likelihood of our intelligence services being able to prevent the release of sarin gas in the Tube, or anthrax in Trafalgar Square, or undetectable poisons into our reservoirs, it is worthwhile looking into the informed criticisms of their American counterparts. These criticisms have been heard since President Jimmy Carter and Admiral Stansfield Turner effectively emasculated the CIA in the late-1970s by sacking top officials who were thought to have behaved illiberally or unethically by using informants with criminal records. Imagine trying to run the Drug Enforcement Administration without ever using former drug-dealers as informants, and you'll understand the problem.

The intelligence expert Mike Waller published an assault on the CIA's decline in effectiveness on 10 September, the day before the attacks. In an article in *Insight* magazine he dwelt on the CIA's 'deteriorated human-intelligence capacity that makes it almost impossible to penetrate key targets and cripples US efforts to detect and prevent terrorist attacks such as the bombings that destroyed two US embassies in Africa and a Navy warship in Yemen'.

The CIA has . . . been forced to admit that it has been making systematic errors about security.

Waller criticized the present director of Central Intelligence George Tenet, a Bill Clinton appointee who is 'a decent fellow but a do-nothing leader when it comes to reform' as part of the problem. Tenet managed to survive into the George W. Bush regime, not least because he was instrumental in renaming the CIA headquarters 'The George Bush Center for Intelligence' after the President's father, who was CIA director (but only from 1976 to 1977).

Despite swallowing a $30 billion annual budget—or perhaps because of it—the American intelligence agencies tend to have bloated management staffs but, as Waller points out, 'relatively few solid linguists, analysts and officers in the field who can accurately and quickly collect and assess raw intelligence from the world's trouble spots'. In Waller's opinion the CIA's rampant politicisation under President Clinton, and its refusal to set severe penalties for security lapses have contributed to a breakdown in morale at Langley. (Tenet's predecessor and former boss John Deutch used

AOL to email highly classified documents from his office to his home.)

Waller also attacks the policy whereby professionals at Langley 'are forced to take sensitivity classes and do role-playing about how stereotypical language and attitudes create a hurtful workplace environment'. The ultra-liberal views of 'a recently-minted counter-intelligence officer in her mid-twenties who had just got her BA in child development' were a particular eye-opener for him.

A lack of Middle Eastern knowledge

A former senior official in the CIA's Directorate of Operations (DO), Reuel Marc Gerecht, takes a similar view. Having served as a field officer in Peshawar on the Pakistan-Afghan border—'the Dodge City of Central Asia', as he puts it—where al-Qa'eda was founded and, until recently, has operated more or less openly, he was horrified by the complacency of his bosses back home who, even after the October 2000 suicide attacks on the embassies and USS *Cole*, claimed that they were 'picking apart' bin Laden's movement 'limb by limb'.

Gerecht warns of the dangers of the CIA's having so few operatives of Middle Eastern background. The Agency depended far too much on Pakistan's Inter-Services Agency, which, though tough and competent, was simply not going to take America's side against al-Qa'eda with anything like the enthusiasm necessary. America has left her strong-men allies in the lurch too often—witness Thieu, Marcos, Somoza, the Shah, Pinochet—for the Pakistani intelligence services to believe that she will do anything for them once their usefulness in the present crisis is over.

'The only way to run offensive counter-terrorist operations against Islamic radicals in more or less hostile territory,' Gerecht warns, 'is with "non-official cover" officers—operatives who are in no way attached to the US government.' Yet, as a former senior Near East Division CIA operative puts it, the Agency 'probably doesn't have a single truly qualified Arabic-speaking officer of Middle Eastern background who can play a believable Muslim fundamentalist, who would volunteer to spend years of his life with shitty food and no women in the mountains of Afghanistan. For Christ's sake, most case officers live in the suburbs of Virginia. We don't do that kind of thing.' A younger colleague of his is equally blunt: 'Ops that involve diarrhoea as a way of life don't happen.'

It might, of course, be that these analysts are merely contributing to the deep cover of an agent high up in the Taleban or al-Qa'eda—one can but hope—but it is much more likely that the increasingly risk-averse nature of American society is being mirrored in its intelligence agencies. Most analysts agree that a complacent National Security Agency has placed far too much reliance on signals intelligence (sigint) and not enough on human intelligence (humint)—i.e., spies in the enemy camp.

If you wish to hear similar complacency over here [in Great Britain], all you need do is listen to former Joint Intelligence Committee chairman Dame Pauline Neville-Jones sticking up for our intelligence services on Radio 4's *Today* programme. 'If you live in a free society,' she said about the scandal that no fewer than 11 suspected terrorists had somehow slipped through Britain, 'you're not very keen for information to be passed between agencies. There's a balance to be struck here.'

Reforms are doubtful

The Joint Intelligence Committee, argues the British intelligence expert and former MoD Middle East desk officer Colonel John Hughes-Wilson, is nonetheless one of the advantages our system has over America's. Author of the 1999 classic, *Military Intelligence Blunders*, Hughes-Wilson is impatient with the way 'the mad alphabet soup of the CIA, the [Defense Intelligence Agency] (DIA), the FBI, the [National Reconnaissance Office] (NRO) and the [National Security Agency] (NSA) are still struggling for mastery' in the United States. He believes that a single controlling organisation is badly needed there, but first the Americans 'have to acknowledge that there is no competitive market economy in intelligence'.

Pessimism is endemic among the analysts about Washington's capacity for the necessary deep-seated reforms. Dr Bruce Hoffmann of the Centre for the Study of Terrorism and Political Violence at St Andrew's University believes that 'it is doubtful that the US or any Western government are adequately prepared to meet the challenge' of 21st-century terrorism. Gerecht goes further and doubts that even given the political will, reform of the CIA is now institutionally possible. He joined the CIA's Directorate of Operations in 1985, but became disillusioned. 'I've long since lost my pride in the DO', he says, 'which has evolved into a sorry blend of *Monty Python* and *Big Brother*'.

Recalling his own eight years in the Near East Division, Gerecht attests that 'not a single Iran desk chief could speak or read Persian. Nor a single Near East Division chief knew Arabic, Persian or Turkish, and only one could get along in French.' Like most other analysts, Gerecht severely doubts whether the CIA has a single humint source in the whole of al-Qa'eda.

Yet this is the organisation which, for the price of some $2 box-cutter knives, $250 air tickets and flying lessons, managed to evade the FBI, hijack four aeroplanes, kill thousands of innocents, humiliate the United States, emasculate Manhattan, threaten major airlines with bankruptcy, and perhaps trigger a global recession. It has to be stopped, even if, as the security and counter-intelligence expert Randy Scheunemann urges, 'a decades-old, self-imposed prohibition on assassination must be revoked and intelligence collection guidelines limiting recruitment of human rights violators should be repealed'. Dirty tricks and assassination might be the only answer, believes Scheunemann, for, as he asks rhetorically, 'How does the CIA propose to penetrate cells made up of individuals who forged their ties over decades in the dust of Palestinian refugee camps, the chaos of Beirut or the killing fields of Afghanistan?'

12

The CIA Is Successfully Fighting Terrorism

Jim Pavitt

Jim Pavitt is the deputy director for operations at the Central Intelligence Agency.

The Central Intelligence Agency (CIA) was preparing for a war on terrorism long before the September 11, 2001, attacks on New York and Washington, D.C. The agency's failure to stop those attacks was not due to ineffective intelligence gathering but because all but a few people in Saudi terrorist Osama bin Laden's inner circle knew the complete plans. However, the CIA's experience and preparation has helped prevent other acts of terrorism. Terrorist attacks cannot be completely prevented, but with sufficient training and support from President George W. Bush and Congress, the CIA will continue to protect the United States.

The threat that we face today from global terrorism is real, it's immediate, and it is unlike any other we have faced before. I say this from 30 years of experience in an intelligence function.

Terrorism as we face it today does not confine its destruction to far off lands. The events of [September] 11th, 2001, tragically make that clear to all of us. And this war will not end with a peace treaty or with the disappearance of a single state or a government. Nor will it in the end be a war which we conclude we have won. Rather, in my view, it's going to be a war which we will be fighting for a long time to come.

On September 11th our country, the American people and the entire world came face to face with a horrible truth. That truth is that the forces of terror are highly resourceful, they have a level of compartmentation seldom seen, they are extremely determined and they are utterly ruthless. If we allow them to continue what they started, they are going to kill us again.

For the men and women of CIA that truth is familiar. With our partners in law enforcement and our allies around the globe we have been battling terrorism for years.

Excerpted from Jim Pavitt's address to Duke University Law School, April 11, 2002. Copyright © 2002 by Jim Pavitt. Reprinted with permission.

I think it's important to note that we did not discover terrorism on the 12th of September. For many of us the war commenced many, many years earlier.

In 1986, when the Cold War was still a defining fact of political life in the United States of America, the Director of the Central Intelligence Agency created something he called the Counter-Terrorist Center. Now more than 15 years since that the CIA's Counter-Terrorist Center—known to us as CTC—remains a model of America's war against terrorism.

Our task is to preempt, to disrupt and to defeat international terrorism. The guiding principle and that which has given us the success we've had to date is agility and flexibility. The Counter-Terrorist Center has become something of great value I think to our country and to the fight against global terrorism. It allows us to use the resources at CIA, the FBI, the Secret Service, a variety of other federal agencies for a couple of specific purposes—to improve our collection and our analysis of intelligence.

In CTC what we do is bring expertise under one roof and then leverage all the other resources in the American and foreign intelligence communities with whom we have relationships to the end of attacking terrorism. Today in CTC, in CIA we have FBI agents working side by side with CIA officers. And by doing so we improve the ability to get the right information to the right people so we can do something about the attacks to come.

Knowledge before the attack

Analysts in the intelligence world, in my field case officers as we call them, operations officers, combine their talents and their diverse experiences to the end of getting us a fuller picture of both the terrorist threat, the terrorist mentality, and they help us to create well-informed strategies for fighting it. We've had a number of significant successes over the years, but the fact remains, and I think it's important that I cite this, that we in the government of the United States as a whole could neither prevent or precisely predict the devastating tragedy of the September 11th attacks. Why do I say that? I believe the answer to the question lies in the very nature of the target itself. On September 10th we were devoting more and more resources against the terrorist target than at any other intelligence challenge we faced. Let me tell you what we knew on the 10th of September.

We had very, very good intelligence of the general structure and strategies of the al Qaeda terrorist organization. We knew and we warned that al Qaeda was planning a major strike. There need be no question about that. What didn't we know?

We never found the tactical intelligence, never uncovered the specifics that could have stopped those tragic strikes that we all remember so well. And as a reality of that difficult and often frustrating fight against terror, the terror cells that we're going up against are typically small and all terrorist personnel in those cells, participating in those cells, perpetrating the acts of terror, all those personnel were carefully screened. The number of personnel who know vital information, targets, timing, the exact methods to be used had to be smaller still.

Some of you out there may have heard [terrorist Osama] bin Laden himself speak about this on that shocking videotape that we recovered in

Afghanistan. On that tape when he was speaking to friends as he sat around in a little room, he talks about the fact that some of the hijackers, indeed, some of the most senior members of his inner circle had been kept in the dark about the full extent of that destruction operation that took place in New York and in Washington on the 11th of September. In my business we call that compartmentation. In his business, terror, killing of innocent people, he calls that compartmentation.

Against that degree of control, that kind of compartmentation, that depth of discipline and fanaticism, I personally doubt, and I draw again upon my 30 years of experience in this business, that anything short of one of the knowledgeable inner circle personnel or hijackers turning himself in to us would have given us sufficient foreknowledge to have prevented the horrendous slaughter that took place on the 11th.

Quick and effective responses

While we did not stop the awful carnage that day our years of preparation and our experience allowed us to respond to the challenges of war quickly and effectively. From the moment the second tower was hit in New York, the CIA began to shift resources to both collection and analysis. We knew from the start that our key contribution would come not in numbers but in expertise.

We've built new units and teams around seasoned officers and we drew heavily on the quality that describes clandestine service and the CIA as a whole—initiative and agility.

Teams of my paramilitary operations officers trained not just to observe conditions but if need be to change them, were among the first on the ground in Afghanistan. With a small logistical footprint they came with lightning speed. We were on the ground within days of that terrible attack. They also came with something else. They came with knowledge of local languages, whatever you heard to the contrary notwithstanding, terrain, and politics. Let me be clear. I am extraordinarily proud of my officers. Proud of their accomplishments. More proud still of their courage. In those few days that it took us to get there after that terrible, terrible attack, my officers stood on Afghan soil, side by side with Afghan friends that we had developed over a long period of time, and we launched America's war against al Qaeda.

On September 10th we were devoting more and more resources against the terrorist target than at any other intelligence challenge we faced.

None of this came easy. You cannot learn [the Afghan language] Pushtan overnight, and you can't truly understand the complexities of tribalism, regionalism, and personalism in Afghanistan by reading the newspaper or a learned book. My people learned about this by years of study and years of practice often in difficult, hostile places and yes indeed, on the ground in Afghanistan itself.

If you hear somebody say, and I have, the CIA abandoned

Afghanistan after the Soviets left and that we never paid any attention to that place until September 11th, I would implore you to ask those people how we were able to accomplish all we did since the Soviets departed. How we knew who to approach on the ground, which operations, which warlord to support, what information to collect. Quite simply, we were there well before the 11th of September.

But let's not make any mistake. This is very, very dangerous work—a fact that the best logistical support can never change. As all of you know, the first American to die by enemy action in Afghanistan was a CIA officer. A son from small town America with a wife and three kids, Michael Spann, was working one of the front lines in the fight against terrorism. Exactly one year almost to the day of his death I shook his hand when I graduated him from our basic training program. His spirit, his talent, his courage won him a place as he went off to Afghanistan among my organization's elite. He went there where the risk was because that's where the intelligence was. He sought and collected, prior to his death, vital intelligence for our country. Sadly all his love, promise and service was cut short in a desolate, mud-walled prison. I know far more about that than anyone in this room, but in death, as in life, he embodies the best of our clandestine service, your clandestine service.

I happen to have the honor right now of managing and running it. And Mike would be the first to tell you that there are hundreds more just like him. And that is good news for us all. Whether it's in the back alleys of some hell hole in this world, and there are a lot of those, and I have a lot of my officers operating them, to the dusty fields of Mazar-e-Sharif where Mike died, we go where we have to go, where someone has to go. The information we uncover has meant better security here at home and overseas. Let there be no question about that.

A series of challenges

The challenges of running intelligence operations against a sophisticated and determined global foe, a foe that doesn't wear a uniform and flies no flag, those challenges are daunting but they can and they will be overcome.

In a run-up to the millennium celebrations the CIA warned the President of the United States of serious terrorism conspiracies around the world. We predicted, we told the President, that there would be between five and 15 serious attacks on U.S. soil. But we did much much more than warn. With our allies and our partners around the world we launched immense efforts to counter those threats. Hundreds of terrorists were arrested, multiple cells of terrorism were destroyed. One terrorist cell planned to blow up a hotel, buses and holy sites in both Israel and Jordan. It had also planned to use chemical weapons. The moments of relevant peace we associate with the millennium were not the result of either chance or accident, they were the result clearly of great skill on the part of a good many people and very hard work. Good intelligence stopped terrorism. We knew then just as we know now that al Qaeda and those who would continue its mission of murder were nothing if not resilient. Remember, the World Trade Center was attacked once before. Stripped today of their huge safe haven in Afghanistan, denied their sanctuary with their allies, the Taliban, driven from power, they are trying even as we sit here tonight in the splendor of this site, trying to recruit, recover and attack us again. And attack us again they will. Before and after September 11th the CIA has pursued an elusive, deadly enemy. More than 1,000 extremists that we believe are linked to al Qaeda have been arrested in more than 70 countries since the attacks on the 11th. But despite what sounds like large numbers, staggering success, the fact of the matter is that we are far from finished. There's a good deal more to be done. There's much much more to be done.

Our years of preparation and our experience allowed us to respond to the challenges of war quickly and effectively.

Because the networks of terror are fluid and dynamic, because they learn from their past and from ours—from our past, from our action—I'm not at liberty to describe to you every thing we've done against them. You would not want me to do that. But let me emphasize that what I'm telling you here tonight is just the tip of the iceberg of what American intelligence can do to protect American interests.

Today, I have more spies stealing more secrets than at any time in the history of the CIA. I'm proud of what we do and proud more of those who put their lives on the lines to protect the lives and freedom of others. I ask you to take me at my word. We're stealing more secrets, providing our leadership with more intelligence than we've ever done before.

On the question of terrorism, the information that CIA collects and assesses deals with more than threats and potential attacks against our interests, decisive though that is. Like you, we recognize that terrorism has deep roots and multiple causes that we as a nation must examine thoroughly. It is not enough for us to understand the what and the how of terrorism, we must know why terrorism exists, why it's attractive to some, and why it can spread to others. Every day through unique clandestine reports and careful reasoned intelligence analysis we convey that essential context to our customers starting with the President and then going to the people around him who make American foreign policy.

The war in which our country finds itself now, a war which we did not seek but one we are determined to win, is not a war against a people or a war against a faith. It is a war against a terrible distortion of human and religious values. It's not merely a war to defend our way of life, it's a war to defend life itself. To be sure, despair and disappointment are the raw materials of terror, but its building blocks are ignorance and intolerance. And it is those evils which are fostered by extremists who have nothing to do with genuine piety that produce the fanatical terrorists which can perpetrate the kind of action we saw on the 11th.

To those who preach hate and hopelessness, the murder of innocents is no crime at all. They falsely portray the massacre of ordinary men, women and children of every race and of every creed as a revenge of the powerless against the powerful. It is no such thing. But as we fight the terrorist groups of today we must be, and frankly we have been, careful to avoid the sort of indiscriminate response that would only add to the strengths of terrorists who will strike us tomorrow.

Working together to stop terrorism

At the same time, the world must find a way to come to grips with the roots of terror. I'm an intelligence officer. That's a responsibility for someone else. But for those who do shape policy the challenge is not merely to attack terrorism but to attack the causes of terrorism as well. As President Bush has said, this will be a long and difficult war. Some of the battles are very visible, others are not. But most are waged by a coalition of nations—Muslim and non-Muslim alike, for we all face a common threat—and all share a deep, deep revulsion for the teachings and tactics of terrorism. Alongside with military and diplomatic coalitions, there's something I think very important and that is a global coalition of intelligence services. From around the world, from our allies and our partners, we receive and we share information. We plan operations together and together in many instances we take terrorists off the streets.

I have more spies stealing more secrets than at any time in the history of the CIA.

The cooperation that I've just described is vital and it is growing. And it is, like so many other parts of my profession, ultimately founded on relationships of great competence and great trust.

Now for the hard truth. Despite the best efforts of so much of the world, the next terrorist attack—it's not a question of if, it's a question of when. With so many possible targets and an enemy more than willing to die, the perfect defense isn't possible. If I knew any society that would mount such a perfect defense, devoid as it would be of the liberties that make us great, is not worth defending.

So instead of intelligence perfection, I can promise only our greatest care and our fullest dedication. I promise that. That depends most of all on the men and women who do the work—operations officers. Newspapers describe operations officers as CIA agents. I recruit agents. I'm an operations officer. My operations officers, talented and bold enough to identify and acquire intelligence anywhere in the world are what we need. Analysts, intelligence analysts skilled and knowledgeable enough to see patterns and data where others do not, that's what we need. And finally, we need scientists, engineers, and support officers who are gifted enough to create the conditions and the tools and the technologies that let the operations officers and the analysts excel. I have those officers at CIA and I'm getting more.

After the deep, debilitating cuts of the 1990s, when many thought that the end of the Cold War would bring us a safer, more predictable world, one in which intelligence was not important, a world in which intelligence officers were no longer as necessary, we now continue to rebuild, back to essential strength where we can continue to do what you and others ask me to do. In the Directorate of Operations alone, since just [the mid-1990s] we are training more than 10 times as many operations officers. These are people with qualifications that we need today and tomorrow. They have the education, they have the background, they have the languages and they have the experience in this country and overseas to get this job done.

I [have] never before, however, focused tonight as I am on fighting terrorism because that's what you asked me to talk to you about. That as decisive and important as counter-terrorism may be to our mission, our country needs to focus on other things as well. From emerging powers and rogue states, to counter-proliferation, and narcotic trafficking. At the end of the day I don't get to pick and choose issues. My job is simply, as my boss tells me, cover them all.

In that and so much else CIA is fortunate to enjoy a tremendous amount of [support] in a democracy like ours that's absolutely crucial to my getting the job done. The President has made a commitment to intelligence that in my mind is truly inspiring. Congress, too, has given us the support we need while exercising the oversight that the American people rightly demand. [I'm] equally impressed with the torrent of letters, phone calls and e-mails we've received at CIA daily from the public and around the world. I'd like to share just one of those with you.

One e-mail that we received that stands out came from an 11 year old girl days after the September 11th attack. She wrote, and I quote, "I'm very scared right now. Would you please tell me what you're doing to make things safe? And don't give me any of that crap about classified information." [Laughter] Unquote.

Many have volunteered to join the fight against terrorism and I'm honored to say we continue to bring in the best and the brightest our country has to offer. The outpouring of support has truly been for somebody as hardened as I am to this business, inspiring. Those people coming in are great men and they're great women. And they work in secret on behalf of the American people and in keeping with the highest values of our people. I hope you will always be proud of them. I certainly am.

13

Airport Security Has Not Improved Since the September 11 Terrorist Attacks

Todd Paglia

Todd Paglia is a freelance writer and the campaign director for Forest Ethics, an environmental organization dedicated to protecting endangered forests and ancient rainforests in North America.

Despite the clamor for improved security at American airports since the terrorist attacks of September 11, 2001, air travel in the United States is still threatened by inadequate security. The federal government has adopted few of the proposals suggested for increased security, and those proposals that have been approved are implemented laxly. In addition, many of the security measures that were imposed immediately following the attacks, such as banning curbside check-ins, were rescinded within a month. Airport security is particularly inadequate when it comes to screening checked bags and carry-on luggage. Airports and airlines are not using advanced bomb detection machines to their full capabilities and carry-on bag screeners are poorly paid and lack sufficient training.

On September 23, 2001, Brian Fitzgerald, a thin and cleancut Caucasian man, entered the Seattle airport to fly home to Arizona. He was booked on Southwest Airlines flight 1439 direct to Phoenix. Knowing that security would be tight in the wake of the 9-11 attacks, he showed up early for his 11:45 a.m. flight. Security guards were stopping every vehicle driving up to the terminal. He knew this would take a little extra time, but he was glad to see the armed officers and felt reassured.

Fitzgerald arrived at the security checkpoint for Terminal B with his carry-on backpack, which he placed on the conveyer belt of the x-ray machine. As he walked through the metal detectors, the alarm went off and

From "Fear of Flying: The Political Economy of Airport Security," by Todd Paglia, *Multinational Monitor*, November 2001. Copyright © 2001 by *Multinational Monitor*. Reprinted with permission.

he was asked to step aside. He was frisked and given a thorough going over with a hand-held metal detector. Finding nothing amiss, the airport security screeners allowed him to retrieve his backpack and board the plane.

As Fitzgerald flew to Phoenix, in the bin right above his head, inside the backpack he carried on, was a 6-inch miniature Chinese short-sword that he accidentally smuggled on board. He didn't realize it was in the pack until he got home—and neither did anyone else.

An alarming safety record

Fitzgerald's experience was not unique. *New York Daily News* reporters went to the airports where the 9-11 flights originated and were able to sneak knives and razors onto flights. In total, the *News* team was able to sneak several of the following items on 10 out of the 12 flights they boarded: a camping knife with a 2½ inch blade, a multi-tool with a knife blade, box cutters like the ones used in the terrorist attacks, scissors and pepper spray. More recently, a Nepalese man was stopped at Chicago's O'Hare airport after he had made it through the x-ray checkpoint. He was in possession of seven knives and a stun gun that had somehow escaped detection.

The Fitzgerald and other incidents highlight what air transportation safety advocates say is a startling post-September airline safety record.

While numerous plans have been expounded, regulations and legislation considered and a rhetorical commitment to safety ratcheted up, not much has changed in actual practice. That has safety advocates alarmed.

Lax regulators and a cost-conscious airline industry share responsibility for the dismal state of U.S. airline security.

Two presidential commissions and numerous reports by the Department of Transportation's Inspector General, Congress's General Accounting Office and airline safety advocates have outlined dozens of serious gaps in security procedures over the years: lack of adequate screening for checked bags, access to high-risk areas by catering companies and others lacking security clearance, and inadequate training of x-ray operators, to name a few. A handful of improvements have made their way into law, but the bulk of the proposals for increased security have not been adopted; and even those adopted are often not rigorously implemented.

Lax regulators and a cost-conscious airline industry share responsibility for the dismal state of U.S. airline security, according to safety advocates. The airlines have successfully resisted calls for strengthened safety measures—such as matching checked bags with passengers and not letting a checked bag on without a corresponding passenger—primarily to avoid the additional expense. In the United States, airlines are charged with screening both passengers and luggage. Here too, they have cut costs and corners, with dire potential consequences, according to safety advocates.

"A month after the September attacks, much of the testimony on Capitol Hill is about lowering airline security," says Paul Hudson, executive director of the Washington, D.C.-based Aviation Consumer Action Project (ACAP), "not, as you might expect, about maintaining current standards or increasing them."

Restrictions are fading away

Immediately following the September attacks, the Federal Aviation Administration (FAA) ordered an unprecedented three-day shutdown of commercial air traffic. When commercial flights resumed, the FAA imposed extra security measures—but many of the new restrictions were relaxed soon thereafter. The FAA lifted the ban on curbside check in, for example, less than a week after the attacks. This allows a passenger to check luggage at the curb and thus avoid potential additional screening under the Computer Assisted Passenger Profiling System (CAPPS), a means of selecting high-risk passengers whose bags get elevated scrutiny.

The ban on having commercial airliners carrying unscreened mail and cargo was also lifted. Restrictions that limited the nation's thousands of private aircraft from flying near major metropolitan areas were phased out a little over one month after the September attacks.

The evolving response to September 11 fits a familiar pattern, says Paul Hudson, executive director of the Washington, D.C.-based Aviation Consumer Action Project. After air disasters, he says, "more often than not there is a substitution of plans and proposals for real actions. Then the heat goes down and nothing happens." The post-September 11 restrictions are fading away; and new farther-reaching rules are on hold in Congress, where controversy over federalizing baggage scanners has stalled new safety rules. For now, the most visible change in airport security is the dramatically increased presence of law enforcement officers and national guardsmen. But many security experts see these deployments as cosmetic.

"It's a dog and pony show, these soldiers with Ak-47s, but security isn't much different," says Peter Williamson, vice president with Rapiscan Security Products, makers of airport security inspection equipment. Law enforcement personnel on site may provide some modest deterrent effect, but probably does little to slow determined terrorists.

Screening checked bags

Where changes are perhaps most needed, say safety advocates, is in the handling of checked and carry-on baggage.

The importance of security on checked bags was made apparent over 13 years ago. En route from London to New York in 1988, Pan Am 103 exploded over Lockerbie, Scotland after a bomb was planted in its cargo hold. Two hundred seventy people died in the blast and ensuing crash.

Although many called for the scanning of all checked bags after the Lockerbie explosion, the FAA never mandated advanced bomb screening. It appears that progress on this front will remain slow going after September 11.

Prior to September 11, the FAA had set 2009 as a target for when all checked bags should be screened by advanced machines. The machines, called CT scanners or CTX machines, are able to detect various threats from plastic explosives to more traditional bombs.

Under current rules, air carriers are responsible for operating and maintaining the bomb detection machines purchased by the FAA, but the airlines are not forced to accept them. According to Department of Transportation Inspector General Kenneth Mead, prior to September 11 a major U.S. carrier had one machine while a small airline had four. One airport refused an advanced machine because it did not match the terminal's color scheme. Twenty of the million-dollar machines were sitting in a government warehouse collecting dust, though post–9-11 the FAA has claimed that deployment would once again move forward.

Security experts say at most 5 percent of checked bags are now screened for bombs using the advanced machines.

Of those machines that have been deployed, most are underused. Mead told the House Committee on Transportation and Infrastructure exactly one month after the September attacks that a July 2001 study found that one third of the machines were being used to scan fewer than "225 bags per day, on average, compared to a certified rate of 225 bags per hour."

After 9-11, the FAA required that all airports with advanced bomb detection machines use them continuously, rather than occasionally. But even after the September 11 tragedy, the Inspector General found that at seven high-risk airports the machines were not being used at their capacity. Mead told the Transportation and Infrastructure Committee that "at some locations the machine was not turned on; at others, the machines were on and staffed with screeners, but no baggage was screened."

Security experts say at most 5 percent of checked bags are now screened for bombs using the advanced machines and estimates are as low as one in 10,000.

"Enforcement actions are certainly being looked at" to compel more screening, says Rebecca Trexler of the FAA Public Affairs Department, though she expresses frustration that further motivation would be required in the wake of September 11.

Bag screeners are a weak link

Low wages, little chance for advancement, lack of training and mind-numbing conditions combine to make carry-on bag screeners another weak link in the security system. Training for x-ray machine operators averages around 12 hours—yet experts maintain that they need between 40 and several hundred hours of training to become truly proficient.

Even with well-trained screeners, the job is inherently difficult. If there is a relatively low rate of incident, for example, finding a gun in a carry-on bag once every couple months or even years, the accuracy rate for detection when a dangerous item does appear on the x-ray screen will be low. This is a predictable result, given the difficulty of focusing on x-ray screens with bags rapidly passing by. With high rates of incident—assume a knife or gun is in every few bags—very high detection rates can be achieved. But screeners at airports typically deal with the former not the latter.

The post–9-11 FAA ban on almost all metal objects that might be used as a weapon—everything from nail clippers to sewing needles to scissors—is increasing the frequency of incidents, and almost certainly elevating the attentiveness of screeners.

But attentiveness is not the only challenge. Many potential weapons are hard to detect. "For example, a gun in profile is easy to see," says Peter Williamson, but detecting a gun when it is viewed from the top, with the barrel facing down and the trigger obscured, is much more difficult.

The same problems apply to knives and other potential weapons. A backpack that has been modified so its steel frame can be removed for use as a weapon is even harder—if not impossible—to spot as a weapon.

The airlines, which control carry-on security, are not using available equipment and technologies that would help address or counteract these problems.

For example, threat image projection (TIP) is a software system that imposes a digital image of a dangerous item into a bag being screened, or it creates an entirely fictitious bag containing a dangerous item, in order to keep screeners on their toes and keep accuracy high. It also measures each screener's rate of detection for the imposed images.

This performance data could be used to identify areas for additional training—which the TIP program can also provide.

It could also be used to terminate employees that do not maintain a certain level of proficiency (currently, low performance screeners are neither required to get additional training nor disqualified from operating x-ray machines).

But the FAA does not require use of this technology in a systematic way. TIP has only been activated on a little more than half of the TIP-ready machines, according to the Inspector General. In at least two airports where the program has been activated, a recent Inspector General investigation determined that operators had learned the password and disabled the program during their shifts.

A reluctance to spend money

Providing an adequate level of air traffic safety would "involve commercial losses and inconvenience," says ACAP's Paul Hudson. "This is the transportation business and when security bumps up against convenience, security loses," says Hudson, though in many but not all cases convenience can be maintained at greater airline expense—for example, by hiring more staff to offset delays from additional precautionary measures.

But the airline industry has displayed a long-term reluctance to spend money to enhance safety. It has resisted deploying and using new security technologies, and failed to provide competent and well-trained baggage screeners.

The result, say safety advocates, is a terrible gamble with passengers' well-being.

"No new form of terrorism has ever not been repeated unless there is much heightened security or a strong deterrent," says Hudson.

"Right now we have neither."

14

Infectious Diseases Threaten National Security

Jonathan B. Tucker

Jonathan B. Tucker is the director of the Chemical and Biological Weapons Nonproliferation Program at the Monterey Institute, which monitors the proliferation of chemical and biological weapons and develops solutions for reducing their spread.

The spread of infectious diseases throughout the world threatens American security. In addition to killing 170,000 Americans each year, diseases such as AIDS and tuberculosis cause civil conflict and political instability in countries and regions that are key to U.S. interests, and endanger American citizens and troops living outside the United States. The impact will become more severe in the coming years as millions of children lose one or both parents to AIDS, leading to economic collapse and the marginalization and exploitation of these youth. The United States must work to contain epidemics or risk future military conflicts.

In an increasingly interdependent world, the United States faces an array of new global challenges that transcend the traditional definition of national security. One important example is the resurgence of infectious disease. In the 1960s and 1970s, powerful antibiotic drugs and vaccines appeared to have banished the major plagues from the industrialized world, leading to a mood of complacency and the neglect of programs for disease surveillance and prevention. Over the past few decades, however, infectious diseases have returned with a vengeance.

National and global dangers

Worldwide, 20 well-known maladies, including tuberculosis, malaria, and cholera, have reemerged since 1973 in more virulent or drug-resistant forms or have spread geographically. Over the same period, at least 30 previously unknown diseases have been identified for which no cures exist. Examples include Ebola and other hemorrhagic fevers in Africa, the worldwide AIDS pandemic, Legionnaire's disease, Lyme disease, Hepatitis C, "mad cow disease," Sin Nombre virus, Nipah virus, and new strains of influenza. Although AIDS was not recognized until the 1980s, it now infects some 36 million people worldwide and kills three million annually. Since 1980, the US death rate from infectious diseases has increased by about 4.8 percent per year, compared with an annual decrease of 2.3 percent in the 15 years before 1980. At present, nearly 170,000 US citizens die annually of AIDS and other infections.

Over the next 20 years, emerging and re-emerging infectious diseases will endanger US citizens at home and abroad.

Not only do importations of disease threaten US citizens directly, but devastating epidemics such as AIDS are spawning widespread political instability and civil conflict in countries where the United States has significant interests. The Clinton administration sought to address these challenges by placing public health on a "new security agenda" along with other nontraditional threats such as environmental degradation, dwindling supplies of clean water, global warming, mass migrations of refugees, and overpopulation. In response to critics who questioned the relevance of infectious disease to national security, President Bill Clinton's National Security Advisor Sandy Berger wrote, "[A] problem that kills huge numbers, crosses borders, and threatens to destabilize whole regions is the very definition of a national security threat. . . . To dismiss it as a 'soft' issue is to be blind to hard realities."

In January 2000, the National Intelligence Council supported the Clinton administration's policy by publishing an unclassified National Intelligence Estimate (NIE) assessing the implications of the global spread of infectious diseases for US national security. Packed with sobering statistics, the NIE concludes that over the next 20 years, emerging and re-emerging infectious diseases will endanger US citizens at home and abroad, threaten troops deployed overseas, and exacerbate political and social instability in key countries and regions. This instability, in turn, will contribute to humanitarian emergencies and military conflicts to which the United States may have to respond. The report also warns that the threat of biowarfare and bioterrorism will grow as rogue states and terrorist groups exploit the ease of global travel and communication to pursue their deadly objectives.

Causes of diseases

Multiple factors have facilitated the emergence and spread of infectious diseases. The overuse of antibiotics to enhance the growth of chickens and cattle has contributed to a dramatic increase in drug-resistant microbes at a time when the discovery of new antibiotics has lagged; the settlement of formerly remote jungle areas has brought humans into increased contact with exotic viruses; the rise of megacities in developing countries with poor health systems has created "hot spots" for the evolution of new infectious agents; climate change has led to a shift in the geographical distribution of pathogens and their insect vectors; and the growing volume of cross-border travel and trade associated with globalization has provided new opportunities for microbial "hitchhikers." For example, the West Nile virus, which caused a major outbreak of encephalitis in New York City in the summer of 1999, had never been seen before in the Western Hemisphere and may have been imported by an infected traveler, a migrating bird, or a stray mosquito on an airplane. Viruses also have the potential to mutate into more lethal and contagious forms, as occurred with the Spanish Flu, which killed more than 20 million people around the globe during 1918–1919 and could well strike again.

The NIE develops three alternative scenarios for the global impact of infectious diseases over the next 20 years. An optimistic scenario projects steady progress toward controlling infectious diseases, while a pessimistic scenario foresees little or no progress as AIDS spreads through the vast populations of India, China, the former Soviet Union, and Latin America, and multiple-drug-resistant strains emerge at a faster pace than new drugs and vaccines can be developed. The third, most likely scenario begins with a decade of deterioration as the AIDS pandemic becomes more severe, followed by limited improvement owing to better prevention and control of childhood diseases, new drugs and vaccines, and gradual socioeconomic development.

In the short term, the NIE predicts that, in the hardest-hit countries of the developing and former communist worlds, the persistent burden of infectious disease is likely to aggravate and even provoke economic decay, social fragmentation, and political polarization. Already, the collapse of public health systems in Russia and the former Soviet republics has led to a dramatic rise in HIV infection and drug-resistant tuberculosis in those countries. By 2010, AIDS and malaria combined will reduce the gross domestic products of several sub-Saharan African countries by 20 percent or more, bringing these nations to the brink of economic collapse as they lose the most productive segment of their populations.

An unsettling future

If current trends continue, a decade from now some 41.6 million children in 27 countries will have lost one or both parents to AIDS, creating a "lost generation" of orphans with little hope of education or employment. These young people may become marginalized or easily exploited for political ends, as in the increasingly pervasive phenomenon of the child-soldier, putting AIDS-stricken countries at risk of further economic decay, increased crime, and political instability. The NIE suggests that by the year 2020, AIDS and tuberculosis will account for the overwhelming majority of infectious disease deaths in the developing world. Nevertheless, a somewhat more hopeful picture has emerged in recent months as growing political pressure has led multinational pharmaceutical companies to lower the price of AIDS drugs sold to poor countries.

The NIE on the global infectious disease threat provides unsettling but enlightening reading. It strongly suggests that unless the United States helps to contain the spread of infectious diseases such as AIDS, malaria, and tuberculosis in the developing and former communist worlds, the resulting socioeconomic collapse could require massive infusions of emergency aid and perhaps even the deployment of US troops to restore order. The Bush administration, which unlike its predecessor has shown little interest in nontraditional threats, would do well to heed this warning.

15

America's Telecommunication Networks Are Vulnerable

John C. Wohlstetter

John C. Wohlstetter is a senior fellow at the Discovery Institute, an organization that supports representative government and the free market, where he specializes in technology deregulation.

The terrorist attacks on America on September 11, 2001, revealed that America's security is at risk due to the vulnerability of its telecommunication networks. Computer hardware is vulnerable because switching and routing equipment is often located in a few buildings that are convenient targets for attack. Software's fragility is caused by global accessibility that makes it easy for hostile users to hack into networks. The federal government, in particular the Federal Communications Commission, must alter its policies in order to eliminate these threats to national security.

The atrocities of September 11, 2001, not only revealed the vulnerability of people living and working within America's borders, but also the vulnerability of our high-technology information society. Collapsing with the twin towers was a veritable mother lode of network communications equipment. For want of communications alone, the New York Stock Exchange could not have reopened that terrible week. In the aftermath of the attack, concerns about network reliability (i.e., maintaining connectivity) and security (i.e., protecting the integrity of databases and communications) have intensified greatly.

Two factors amplified the telecommunications vulnerabilities exposed on September 11:

• The vast increase in the Internet user population, and the evolution of the Internet into a form of mass communication.

• Current telecommunications regulatory policies that prefer shared local exchange facilities to separate ones, thus discouraging multiple local facilities.

From "The Vulnerability of Networks," by John C. Wohlstetter, *Regulation*, Winter 2001.
Copyright © 2001 by Cato Institute. Reprinted with permission.

As the United States looks for ways to improve the security of its citizens, government and the telecommunications industry must also find ways to improve the reliability and security of our large and vital communications networks.

Inadequate security

The advent of broad public Internet access has transformed network security by adding vast numbers of users, many of whom have only rudimentary computer skills. That, in turn, has complicated the task of securing networks. The administrator of a private network has authority to control the behavior of users, employing such tools as frequent password changes, limiting access to portions of the network, and restricting access to work-related sites. What is more, private networks once were used primarily by people with a significant amount of general computer knowledge and particular expertise with their own network. That, in turn, provided an additional layer of security by restricting access.

But those security protections are anathema to commercial Internet service providers that compete to attract customers based on their systems' ease-of-use, ready access, and broad interconnectivity. A network is only as secure as its most careless user. And so, public networks are endemically vulnerable to hostile entry. Securing those networks will require implementing special protections as part of the next generation of computer and Internet software. Until now, security has not been a high priority of software designers, and the biggest holes are in the most popular releases. Programmers will plug holes only if consumers demand it. The federal government, as the largest buyer in the software marketplace, can insist on better security and thereby drive developers to respond.

Software's accessibility, global reach, and fragility make for vulnerable systems.

Similar to the Internet, America's public-switched telecommunications networks are, in reality, a web of linked computers with terminals (computers, phones, or faxes) attached at the customers' premises. Voice networks thus share the vulnerabilities of their datanet cousins: In an effort to build systems that are easy to use, readily accessible, and have a broad activity, telecommunications companies (under the jurisdiction of federal regulatory agencies) have built systems that are vulnerable to deliberate attack. To decrease that vulnerability, significant changes must be made to both the system's hardware and software.

Network plant vulnerabilities primarily arise out of physical proximity. Switching and routing equipment that provide the telecommunications backbone for a geographic area often are located in just a few buildings, making an easy target for attack. That fact was underscored on September 11 when the World Trade Center collapse knocked out a telecommunications facility in Lower Manhattan that supplied 80 percent of the New York Stock Exchange's communications capacity. That was not the nation's first experience with such a failure: In May of 1998, the destruction of a single station in the Chicago suburb of Hinsdale, Ill., knocked out the facilities of several major carriers.

The May 1998 incident and the September 11 attack underscore a simple truth for communications infrastructure technologists: You cannot build a smart network with dumb buildings. Despite the growth of local loop entry following the passage of the 1996 Telecommunications Act, network concentration has persisted. Federal Communications Commission (FCC) data show that, between 1990 and 1999, the total number of Bell central offices rose by one percent to 9,968, while total phone lines they serve jumped 34 percent. As for Bell's rivals, one study shows that less than 10 percent of competing carriers have facilities fully separate from Bell networks.

Software's fragility

Even more worrisome than the vulnerability of hardware is that of software. Software is global, programmable, accessible, and fragile. Its global reach means that widely separate geographic hardware infrastructure nodes can all crash if controlled by a unitary software superstructure that fails. Programmable features give network software enormous flexibility to control and reconfigure hardware, but such power potentially is available to all users (including those with malevolent intentions) who have the skill to bypass network firewalls. Open access means that hostile users have access to network innards that in earlier times were beyond user reach. And software's fragility makes fixing it a demanding task.

As an example of the software vulnerability of telecommunications networks, consider the AT&T network crash on Martin Luther King Day, 1990. A single punctuation mark at the end of a single line of software code (in a multimillion-line code switch) caused AT&T to lose over half of its long distance capacity in 19 minutes, on one of the busiest calling days of the year. AT&T's network-signaling software controlled switching hardware dispersed nationwide. Programmed mistakenly, the software altered how the network worked, and not for the better: It crashed. And that failure was the result of a simple programming mistake; one can only imagine the results of an attack engineered to produce the broadest possible effect.

The FCC and other federal agencies must alter their regulations and policies . . . to promote reliability and security.

In essence, software represents a kind of Information-Age Faustian bargain: Hardware controlled by software is vastly more flexible than the old-time systems of pure hardware because the contemporary systems are reconfigurable in real-time, thus offering users many options. But software's accessibility, global reach, and fragility make for vulnerable systems. It will take consequential advances in software architectures—e.g., partitioning of dual software systems to support hardware, to break that bargain—and that will be no easy task.

What remedies might be proposed for such vulnerabilities? Perhaps the best would be for networks to embrace an old piece of conventional wisdom: Never rely on one of anything. From a hardware standpoint, physical geographic diversity is essential; new local loop plants would decrease the possibility of broad disruptions in telecommunications from the destruction of a single facility. The industry could also use technology diversity to complement spatial diversity: Wireless and wireline could provide mutual redundancy.

Turning to software, diversity also would be valuable. The 1990 AT&T network crash showed that a single-point software failure can be as devastating as any hardware failure. Today's commercial software is riddled with security holes, including "backdoors" unknown to most users but exploited by hackers. It would be far better for industry to build added robustness and adaptability into networks to enable rapid return to normal should a disruption occur. It is the equivalent of the Cold War strategy of hardening missile silos so as to withstand a first strike, preserving a retaliatory capability. Telecom networks can be remarkably resilient if built wisely.

Improving FCC policies

The FCC came to network reliability reluctantly. Neither the Martin Luther King Day AT&T crash nor several Bell company network crashes in the summer of 1991 spurred the agency to act. It took an AT&T outage in September 1991 that shut down LaGuardia Airport (leaving two FCC commissioners stranded on the tarmac) to get the agency's attention.

Prodded by Congress, the FCC established the first Network Reliability Council, convened early in 1992. In all, there have been five panels, each focusing on accidental outages (the fourth and fifth panels were named Network Reliability and Interoperability Council—NRIC). The most recent panel met October 30, 2001, and hired reports on damage and recovery after the September 11 attacks. A new NRIC will be convened this January (the panels have a statutory two-year lifespan, per the Federal Advisory Committee Act), with homeland security, no doubt, slated to be its prime focus.

FCC policies since the AT&T divestiture have endeavored to promote the entry of competitors into the local loop market, a process intensified by passage of the 1996 Telecommunications Act. Unfortunately, those policies have exacerbated the vulnerabilities discussed above: Encouraging the sharing of local loop facilities—e.g., switching centers, lines, cell towers, mobile telephone switching offices—has concentrated multiple carriers into single locations, providing attackers with attractive targets. Limiting incumbent carriers' ability to control access to their facilities (in an effort to prevent the incumbents from limiting competitor access to shared facilities) has increased the chance of successful penetration of network facilities. Promoting the use of open network architecture to facilitate network access for competitors has also increased the opportunities for malicious users to penetrate network systems. Making matters worse, the FCC has allocated only 189 MHz of spectrum for domestic wireless use (as compared to over 300 MHz in several European countries and Japan), thus limiting the use of wireless hardware to diversify telecommunications infrastructure.

The FCC and other federal agencies must alter their regulations and policies to address those shortcomings and to promote reliability and security. Among the changes that should be considered:

• Implement policies to encourage competitors to build their own facilities instead of continuing to share facilities with the local Bells.

• Allow incumbent firms to vet all personnel with access to sensitive facilities—perhaps using biometric authentication and security checks—to prevent penetration by malevolent agents.

• Allocate additional spectrum that was dedicated to high-definition television, thus enabling the U.S. domestic cellular spectrum to match European allocations. That would enhance backup reserves greatly, and also would increase wireless capacities during an emergency. (Wireless optics that are being deployed in Manhattan as part of the post-September 11 restoration will also help.)

• Amend tax law to accelerate depreciation of existing plants, and apply rapid write-off to investment in redundant critical network components.

• Implement service priority procedures (designating which users have priority in a crisis—police, fire, medical, etc.) that ration capacity in large urban areas.

• Promote broadband deployment by exempting new technology investment from regulation, including in the local loop. With enough new broadband capacity, there would be no need for priority rationing.

• Act as a trusted intermediary for the sharing of sensitive network information, in order to improve inter-network operations in the event of disaster or attack.

Above all, enhancing network reliability and security will require the market interactions of customers demanding access redundancy and service suppliers deploying duplicative assets to meet the demand. Just as no Wall Street firm that moves back to Lower Manhattan will rely on a single connection anymore, so businesses nationwide will add backup for key network assets (just as they did prior to Y2K). The FCC can further help by more deregulation, especially concerning the local loop. Software solutions will have to be largely customer-driven, as suppliers show little sign of fixing things on their own. As for the human element of security, getting people to not use "mom" as their password may prove the biggest challenge of all.

Organizations to Contact

The editors have compiled the following list of organizations concerned with the issues debated in this book. The descriptions are derived from materials provided by the organizations. All have publications or information available for interested readers. The list was compiled on the date of publication of the present volume; the information provided here may change. Be aware that many organizations take several weeks or longer to respond to inquiries, so allow as much time as possible.

American Civil Liberties Union (ACLU)
125 Broad St., 18th Floor, New York, NY 10004-2400
(212) 549-2500
e-mail: aclu@aclu.org • website: www.aclu.org

The American Civil Liberties Union is a national organization that works to defend Americans' civil rights guaranteed by the U.S. Constitution, arguing that measures to protect national security should not compromise fundamental civil liberties. It publishes and distributes policy statements, pamphlets, and press releases with titles such as "In Defense of Freedom in a Time of Crisis" and "National ID Cards: 5 Reasons Why They Should Be Rejected."

American Enterprise Institute (AEI)
1150 17th St. NW, Washington, DC 20036
(202) 862-5800 • fax: (202) 862-7177
website: www.aei.org

The American Enterprise Institute for Public Policy Research is a scholarly research institute that is dedicated to preserving limited government, private enterprise, and a strong foreign policy and national defense. It publishes books including *Study of Revenge: The First World Trade Center Attack and Saddam Hussein's War Against America*. Articles about terrorism and September 11 can be found in its magazine, *American Enterprise*, and on its website.

Brookings Institution
1775 Massachusetts Ave. NW, Washington, DC 20036
(202) 797-6000 • fax: (202) 797-6004
e-mail: brookinfo@brook.edu • website: www.brookings.org

The institution, founded in 1927, is a think tank that conducts research and education in foreign policy, economics, government, and the social sciences. In 2001 it began America's Response to Terrorism, a project that provides briefings and analysis to the public and which is featured on the center's website. Other publications include the quarterly *Brookings Review*, periodic *Policy Briefs*, and books including *Terrorism and U.S. Foreign Policy*.

Cato Institute
1000 Massachusetts Ave. NW, Washington, DC 20001-5403
(202) 842-0200 • fax: (202) 842-3490
e-mail: cato@cato.org • website: www.cato.org

The institute is a nonpartisan public policy research foundation dedicated to limiting the role of government and protecting individual liberties. It publishes the quarterly magazine *Regulation*, the bimonthly *Cato Policy Report*, and numerous policy papers and articles. Works on terrorism include "Does U.S. Intervention Overseas Breed Terrorism?" and "Military Tribunals No Answer."

Center for Defense Information
1779 Massachusetts Ave. NW, Suite 615, Washington, DC 20036
(202) 332-0600 • fax: (202) 462-4559
e-mail: info@cdi.org • website: www.cdi.org

The Center for Defense Information is a nonpartisan, nonprofit organization that researches all aspects of global security. It seeks to educate the public and policymakers about issues such as weapons systems, security policy, and defense budgeting. It publishes the monthly publication *Defense Monitor*, the issue brief "National Missile Defense: What Does It All Mean?" and the studies "Homeland Security: A Competitive Strategies Approach" and "Reforging the Sword."

Center for Immigration Studies
1522 K St. NW, Suite 820, Washington, DC 20005-1202
(202) 466-8185 • fax: (202) 466-8076
e-mail: center@cis.org • website: www.cis.org

The Center for Immigration Studies is the nation's only think tank dedicated to research and analysis of the economic, social, and demographic impacts of immigration on the United States. An independent, nonpartisan, nonprofit research organization founded in 1985, the center aims to expand public support for an immigration policy that is both pro-immigrant and low-immigration. Among its publications are the backgrounders "The USA PATRIOT Act of 2001: A Summary of the Anti-Terrorism Law's Immigration-Related Provisions" and "America's Identity Crisis: Document Fraud Is Pervasive and Pernicious."

Chemical and Biological Arms Control Institute (CBACI)
1747 Pennsylvania Ave. NW, 7th Floor, Washington, DC 20006
(202) 296-3550 • fax: (202) 296-3574
e-mail: cbaci@cbaci.org • website: www.cbaci.org

CBACI is a nonprofit corporation that promotes arms control and nonproliferation, with particular focus on the elimination of chemical and biological weapons. It fosters this goal by drawing on an extensive international network to provide an innovative program of research, analysis, technical support, and education. Among the institute's publications is the bimonthly report *Dispatch* and the reports "Bioterrorism in the United States: Threat, Preparedness, and Response" and "Contagion and Conflict: Health as a Global Security Challenge."

Federal Aviation Administration (FAA)
800 Independence Ave. SW, Washington, DC 20591
(800) 322-7873 • fax: (202) 267-3484
website: www.faa.gov

The Federal Aviation Administration is the component of the U.S. Department of Transportation whose primary responsibility is the safety of civil aviation. The FAA's major functions include regulating civil aviation to promote safety and fulfill the requirements of national defense. Among its publications are *Technology Against Terrorism, Air Piracy, Airport Security, and International Terrorism: Winning the War Against Hijackers* and *Security Tips for Air Travelers.*

Institute for Policy Studies (IPS)
733 15th St. NW, Suite 1020, Washington, DC 20005
(202) 234-9382 • fax: (202) 387-7915
website: www.ips-dc.org

The Institute for Policy Studies is a progressive think tank that works to develop societies built around the values of justice and nonviolence. It publishes reports including *Global Perspectives: A Media Guide to Foreign Policy Experts.* Numerous articles and interviews on September 11 and terrorism are available on its website.

National Security Agency
9800 Savage Rd., Ft. Meade, MD 20755-6248
(301) 688-6524
website: www.nsa.gov

The National Security Agency coordinates, directs, and performs activities, such as designing cipher systems, which protect American information systems and produce foreign intelligence information. It is the largest employer of mathematicians in the United States and also hires the nation's best codemakers and codebreakers. Speeches, briefings, and reports are available on its website.

United States Department of State, Counterterrorism Office
Office of Public Affairs, Room 2507
U.S. Department of State
2201 C St. NW, Washington, DC 20520
(202) 647-4000
e-mail: secretary@state.gov • website: www.state.gov

The office works to develop and implement American counterterrorism strategy and to improve cooperation with foreign governments. Articles and speeches by government officials are available on its website.

Bibliography

Books

Yonah Alexander and   *Usama bin Laden's Al-Qaida: Profile of a Terrorist Network.*
Michael S. Swetnam   Ardsley, NY: Transnational, 2001.

Robert Baer   *See No Evil: The True Story of a Ground Soldier in the CIA's War on Terrorism.* New York: Crown, 2002.

Cabel Carr   *The Lessons of Terror: A History of Warfare Against Civilians: Why It Has Always Failed and Why It Will Fail Again.* New York: Random House, 2002.

Anthony H.   *Terrorism, Asymmetric Warfare, and Weapons of Mass Destruction: Defending the U.S. Homeland.* Westport, CT: Praeger, 2002.
Cordesman

James X. Dempsey   *Terrorism and the Constitution: Sacrificing Civil Liberties in the Name of National Security.* Washington, DC: First Amendment Foundation, 2002.
and David Cole

Steven Emerson   *American Jihad: The Terrorists Living Among Us.* New York: Free Press, 2002.

Peter D. Feaver and   *Soldiers and Civilians: The Civil-Military Gap and American National Security.* Cambridge, MA: MIT Press, 2001.
Richard H. Kohn, eds.

Kathlyn Gay   *Silent Death: The Threat of Chemical and Biological Terrorism.* Brookfield, CT: Twenty-First Century Books, 2001.

Philip B. Heymann   *Terrorism and America: A Commonsense Strategy for a Democratic Society.* Cambridge, MA: MIT Press, 1998.

James F. Hoge and   *How Did This Happen?: Terrorism and the New War.* New York: PublicAffairs, 2001.
Gideon Rose, eds.

Misha Klein and   *September 11, Contexts and Consequences: An Anthology.* Berkeley, CA: Copy Central, 2001.
Adrian McIntyre, eds.

Harvey W. Kushner   *Terrorism in America: A Structured Approach to Understanding the Terrorist Threat.* Springfield, IL: Charles C. Thomas, 1998.

Philip M. Melanson   *Secrecy Wars: National Security, Privacy, and the Public's Right to Know.* Washington, DC: Brassey's, 2001.

Paul R. Pillar   *Terrorism and U.S. Foreign Policy.* Washington, DC: Brookings Institution Press, 2001.

Jeffrey D. Simon   *The Terrorist Trap: America's Experience with Terrorism.* Bloomington: Indiana University Press, 2001.

Strobe Talbott and   *The Age of Terror: America and the World After September 11.* New York: Basic Books, 2001.
Nayan Chanda, eds.

Raymond Tanter   *Rogue Regimes: Terrorism and Proliferation.* New York: St. Martin's Press, 1998.

Periodicals

America   "The Bush Doctrine," March 18, 2002.

Daniele Archibugi   "Toward a Global Rule of Law," *Dissent,* Spring 2002.
and Iris Young

Ronald Brownstein   "Green Light, Red Light," *American Prospect,* November 19, 2001.

Valerie L. Demmer   "Civil Liberties and Homeland Security," *Humanist,* January/February 2002.

Jamie Dettmer   "Security Measures Leave Many Airsick," *Insight on the News,* April 22, 2002.

John M. Deutch and   "Smarter Intelligence," *Foreign Policy,* January/February
Jeffrey H. Smith   2002.

Economist   "Time for a Rethink," April 20, 2002.

George P. Fletcher   "War and the Constitution," *American Prospect,* January 1, 2002.

Michael J. Glennon   "Preempting Terrorism," *Weekly Standard,* January 28, 2002.

Brian Hansen   "Intelligence Reforms," *CQ Researcher,* January 25, 2002.

Scott Harris   "Freedom Fighters of the Digital World," *Los Angeles Times Magazine,* January 13, 2002.

Charles Lane   "In Pursuit of Terrorism," *Washington Post National Weekly Edition,* December 3–9, 2001.

Patrick Marshall   "Policing the Borders," *CQ Researcher,* February 22, 2002.

David Moberg   "Every Breath You Take," *In These Times,* October 29, 2001.

Mackubin Owens   "Bomb Blocking," *American Enterprise,* April/May 2001.

Phyllis Schlafly Report   "Security Starts at Our Borders," November 2001.

Jeffrey Rosen   "Silicon Valley's Spy Game," *New York Times Magazine,* April 14, 2002.

William J. Taylor   "Is the Military Prepared?" *World & I,* December 2001.

Steven Weinberg   "Can Missile Defense Work?" *New York Review of Books,* February 14, 2002.

Jason Zengerle   "Infinite Justice," *New Republic,* November 19, 2001.

Index

Student and Exchange Visitor
Information System (SEVIS), 41–42
Sudan, 51
sunset clauses, 25, 26, 30
Supreme Court
exclusion of aliens and, 45
imposition of martial rule and, 58
indefinite detention of alien residents
and, 44
unlawful combatants and, 58–59, 62

Taliban, 9, 49, 50
Taylor, William J., 9
technology
advances in, require changes in
legislation, 25
detection and
automated fingerprint identification
system and, 38
bombs and, 86–87
Computer Assisted Passenger
Profiling System (CAPPS), 86
scanners, 10
intelligence agencies should upgrade,
10
outpaces legislation, 25
sunset clauses and, 30
threat image projection, 88
see also Internet
telecommunications
AT&T, 95, 96
regulatory policies for, 93, 97
security is not priority of designers of,
94
see also Internet
Telecommunications Act (1996), 96
temporary workers, 40–41
Tenet, George, 74
terrorists
are automatically war criminals, 51
con, 57
are too broadly defined in USA
PATRIOT Act, 29
arrest of, 81
criminal-law response to described, 49,
55
destruction of cells by Central
Intelligence Agency, 80
federal courts should prosecute, 57
con, 50
fluid nature of organization of, 81
perfect defense against, is impossible,
82
preemptive measures against, 50
prosecution of, by International
Criminal Tribunal for Yugoslavia
(ICTY), 54–55
recruitment of, 19
regimes that sponsor, 14

danger from, is overstated, 70
use foreign students as agents, 41
should be prosecuted by military
constitutional protections do not
apply, 51–52
is matter of national security, 49–50
training camps for, 14
visas for, 40–41
win if we restrict civil liberties, 32
threat image projection (TIP), 88
Trexler, Rebecca, 87
Tucker, Jonathan B., 89
Turner, Stansfield, 74

UN Human Rights Commission, 60
Uniting and Strengthening America by
Providing Appropriate Tools Required
to Intercept and Obstruct Terrorism
Act. *See* USA PATRIOT Act
unlawful combatants, 58–59, 61, 62
U.S. Agency for International
Development (USAID), 21
USA PATRIOT Act
alien residents are focus of, 24
defines terrorists too broadly, 29
enactment of, 23
full name of, 25
has updated existing legislation, 25, 26
Internet and, 29–30
provisions of
deportation, 45
detention, 44–45
exclusion, 45
sunset clauses in, 25, 26
threatens civil liberties, 29–30
"U.S. Military Transformation: Not Just
More Spending But Better Spending"
(CDI), 11
USS *Cole*, 75

visas
are too easy to obtain, 36
for foreign students, 40–42
waiver of, 39–40
vital records, 37–38, 39

Waller, Mike, 74, 75
Washington Post (newspaper), 51
Watson, Dale, 41
White, Mary Jo, 50
Williams, Paul R., 48
Williamson, Peter, 86, 88
wiretaps, 25, 29
Wohlstetter, John C., 93
World War II
Japanese Americans during, 32, 47
saboteurs during, 58

Zadvydas case, 44